D1520826

The Emily Post Book of

ETIQUETTE FOR YOUNG PEOPLE

The Emily Post book of

# ETIQUETTE FOR
# YOUNG PEOPLE

by Elizabeth L. Post

FUNK & WAGNALLS · NEW YORK

# Contents

2979

vi   *Contents*

# The Why and Wherefore

The why and wherefore of writing a book about manners for young people is perfectly simple. For better or worse, the world is run by adults, and until that changes you'll have to get along with them—as well as with each other. That's the "why." The "wherefore" is that certain basic suggestions or rules—whatever you want to call them—will make life easier for you and everyone around you. Etiquette isn't a set of stuffy, rigid regulations; it is good common sense linked to thoughtfulness for others, and its purpose is to make you more attractive and easy to get along with. You'll find that if you make these "rules" a part of your personality they'll help you become more popular and get more fun out of being with, not only older people, but your own age group too.

No sensible adult expects teen-agers to conform exactly to his idea of how things should be done—neither the little things like how you wear your hair nor the big things like how to fight a war. But adults do have the greatest confidence that you will adhere to certain basic principles, and the least painful way to learn them is for someone to teach you. By "someone" I mean parents, teachers, clergymen, and all the other adults you come into contact with.

Believe it or not, etiquette—or good manners, if you like that phrase better—is one of those basic principles. Rules of good behavior have been built up over hundreds of years; worthless ones are continually being discarded and those proven to be useful are kept and improved upon. All of this doesn't mean much to anyone about to become a teen; all he's interested in is getting away from mother's apron strings and he doesn't much care how he does it. But by the time he's come out at the other end—seventeen, eighteen, or nineteen years old—and has a year or two of college under his belt, he probably will begin to see the value of experience, education, and some of these principles.

In writing this book for you, my aim is to make the whole business of becoming an adult easier and more fun. Everyone, whether he admits it or not, wants a feeling of confidence, and you just won't have it unless you know what you're doing. The real problem is this: how does one learn the right way to behave in hundreds of different, and occasionally difficult, situations? I'm sure your parents would be the best teachers if you'd listen to them. But sometimes you don't, and sometimes it's possible that they and other adults don't do their job properly. So I'm hoping that you'll be wise enough to look for the answers in a book. And that is mainly why I have written this book: to provide answers to your questions.

# ETIQUETTE
# BEGINS
# AT HOME

# 1 Your Family

Suddenly, you're almost an adult! It happened so fast that you—and your parents—can't understand it, but all at once you are faced with a whole new set of problems. More than anything else, you want to emerge from constant supervision, to become independent, and to choose a social life of your own. And yet, because you are constantly confronted with new situations, you need the guidance and support of your parents. You are, in a sense, betwixt and between, and while the condition brings the fun of entering an adult world, it brings the trials as well. Etiquette, by giving you a guideline on how to act in almost every situation involving contact with other people, provides a bridge. Not only a bridge between you and your parents, but a bridge between your old childhood world and the world you are entering.

Your parents must try to realize this too, and I wish you would get them to look over this chapter with you. Getting along during these transition years is a bumpy two-way street, full of pitfalls, and while you're "in between," you and your mother and father should realize that, though you do need some supervision, you should also be encouraged, with their help, to make your own decisions.

Courtesy begins at home. If you practice your manners with your family and the guests who come to your house, you'll never have any problem when you're in other homes, or among strangers. It's very hard, in fact practically impossible, not to relax and let down on some of the formalities at home; besides, life would be difficult if you didn't. But leaving the formalities aside, you can still stick to the basic principles of unselfishness and consideration, and that's what etiquette is.

Your parents are older and, whether you believe it or not, wiser than you. I don't mean you can't do some things better than they can, but in just plain living experience they're way ahead. Therefore, no matter how at odds with them you may feel at times, you must respect their advice and decisions. They, in turn, should not expect blind obedience; you have reached the age when your opinions are entitled to attention and respect.

## Your Parents

The manner in which you speak to your parents is important. Call them "Mom" and "Dad" or whatever derivative of "Mother" and "Father" you prefer. But please, please don't call them by their first names, or by cute nicknames which might imply any sort of disrespect.

The tone of your voice is a dead giveaway. A long-suffering "What now?" note in your voice every time your mother calls you can effectively cut off all communication. A reasonably cheerful

"What is it, Dad?" or "What do you want, Mom?" tells them you're willing to cooperate—and if you are so are they.

Your attitude when your parents say "No" can make life easier or harder. Save your ammunition for important things. If you don't put up an argument or make a crisis out of *every* adverse decision they hand down, they'll be much more willing to listen when you ask calmly, not hysterically, for a really important permission. If only for tactical reasons, don't pull out that overdone "But everyone else does!" line. It's like rubbing sandpaper on an exposed nerve and it won't—and shouldn't—work. Think up your own good reasons. If your argument is sound, and not based entirely on the fact that this is the current practice or fad, you'll have a much better chance of winning parental approval.

If you're a boy, treat your mother with as much respect as you would any other lady, or even more. Open doors for her, hold her chair at the table, and offer to carry heavy parcels or move furniture. Remember, too, she's human and an occasional compliment from a son (or daughter) more than makes up for a lot of difficult times.

Don't brood over real or imagined injustice. Frankness and communication are vital to family harmony. If you have a beef, out with it! Often your parents don't even know why you've been going around for three days with a face like a thunderstorm. The reverse is true too. When your father has been grouchy for a couple of days, it's easy to convince yourself that he's annoyed with you. Instead of brooding about it, a simple "What's the matter, Dad—did I do something?" will clear the air. If you did, it will open the way to talking it out. More than likely he'll say, "No, we just lost an important sale at the office," and, although you can't help, it will ease the tension for you—and other members of the family—to know the cause lies outside your home. Airing problems has always been the best way to solve, or at least, diminish them.

## Your Brothers and Sisters

The fact that they live under the same roof and can't avoid each other doesn't mean that brothers and sisters *always* like each other. You may, of course, be very close to one or another member of your family, or you may not. But, however you feel, if you recognize that they are individuals with just as many problems as you have, that their likes and dislikes may not be similar to yours, and that they have the right to share your parents' affections with you, family relations will run much more smoothly.

Try to keep jealousy and envy out of your make-up. It's not easy when sister Sue has gorgeous blond hair, or brother Pete is the star on every team at school. But it's a challenge, and if you can meet it by developing some asset of your own that they don't have, you'll do a lot of growing up in the process.

Privacy is terribly important. Diaries and letters are inviolable—they may never be opened or read without the owner's permission. Telephone calls are too. Listening in on sister's conversation on another extension may be an entertaining diversion for brother, but it violates every rule of decent behavior.

"Squealing" is inexcusable. If you know that, against your parents' wishes, your brother lights up a cigarette the minute he leaves the house, talk to him about it if you want to, but don't snitch to your parents. It's his problem, and being your brother's keeper does not mean telling your parents about his behavior. Tattletales effectively and quickly kill any rapport between themselves and other members of their families.

Stay away from your brother's or sister's parties unless you're really urged to be there. Whether he's older or younger, it's his right to entertain only his own group if he wishes, and your presence can be a real annoyance.

Teasing younger brothers and sisters is not only fun, but a certain amount of it is probably good for them if you know when to stop. When you hear that note of desperation or see the hint of a tear, quit, right then and there. Little ones all love horseplay, but they'll love you much more if you recognize when they've had enough.

## Your Parents' Friends

When older guests come to your house, they should be treated with more of that same respect you show your parents. It's a great chance to practice your manners: pretend you're an assistant host or hostess and try out various kinds of warm greetings. I love to go to houses where the young people, when they hear my voice, come to the hall with a friendly "Hi, Mrs. Post, how've you been?" Or, "Did you have a good summer?" Or, "What's Cindy been doing?" A prompt, firm handshake rather than a nod, after an introduction, puts everyone at ease. Incidentally, if you have friends with you who are strangers to your parents' visitors, there is no better time to practice introductions than with close family friends. You don't, of course, want to intrude too long, but you really should stay around and chat for just a few minutes. Young people who struggle slowly out of a chair, grunt a brief "Hi" when they are introduced, and escape as rapidly as possible from a situation that is obviously a great bore to them are scarcely making themselves very attractive. Imagine how you'd feel if you said "Hello" to a friend's mother and she greeted you in a tone which clearly said, "Oh, no—you again. I thought you'd be in school." Well, when you give a cursory, bored "Hello" to your parents' visitors, they are left with exactly the same feeling—and it's not one of admiration or affection!

## Family Secrets

Every family has certain things it doesn't wish discussed or even mentioned in public. It may be a financial matter, it may be about an illness, or it may be a personal relationship, but no one—parent or child—has any right to talk about these things to anyone. Even a best friend should not be trusted with information that has been labeled "top secret" or about which a brother or sister has asked, "Please don't tell."

It's unfair to burden friends with family secrets. If someone asks, "Is it true the McDonalds are in trouble?" it's much easier for that friend if he can honestly say, "I have no idea." Otherwise, he may be forced into fibbing for you. And if the secret does leak out, and your family finds out how, not only you, but your friend, will be on the black list.

## Family Pride

Build up your family to other people. No one admires a person who constantly criticizes his relatives, and don't forget that since you are a member of the family your remarks reflect on *you* too. How would you like to be greeted by a friend of your parents with: "Oh, Jim, I hear you just dropped back a grade"? Naturally you would be hurt and resentful that your mother or father had been spreading the unflattering news to their acquaintances. We all have faults and problems, and there is no sense broadcasting those of our family or friends. Remember the famous saying "United we stand, divided we fall"? Well, it applies to a family also. A family is a team; remember that and life at home will be a lot more fun.

# 2 Your Possessions

We all value most the things that are hard to come by. We may thoroughly enjoy the possessions we have as children, and to some extent even appreciate them, but most of us don't truly value what we have until we begin to realize its worth, and in some cases to recognize the difficulty of acquiring it. This realization leads to an awakening desire to take care of one's things. When you were a child, let's say you were given a Brownie camera. You lost it on your first day at summer camp and your mother promptly sent you another. You dropped that one in the lake before the summer was over. Easy come, easy go. Now, things are different. Not only are the things you receive worth more in dollars and cents, but you are old enough to understand their value, and the sacrifice that may be involved in the gift. This is even truer if you have skimped and saved to buy the article yourself.

One of the first things of very great importance to you may well be the money you earn, or that you are given as an allowance.

## *Money Matters*

Every boy and girl should have some money of his own to do with exactly as he wishes. Families who can afford it generally give teen-agers some allowance, free and clear, with no strings attached. This can be augmented by part-time or summer jobs. As to the actual amounts for allowances, it is impossible to say because requirements vary so in different areas, as do family circumstances. A city boy needs more cash—every time he takes a bus or subway it costs him something, while his country cousin is riding the same distance on a bicycle. Prices are higher, too, in the city. Movies, food, and entertainment are much bigger budget items than in the country. The country boy might take his date to a square dance for fifty cents or so, while the city boy, if he wishes to dance, must go to a night club or dance hall where the admission or cover charge may be as high as several dollars.

A possible scale for a weekly allowance, necessarily subject to change to fit the circumstances, might run something like this:

13–14 years   $1–$2
15–17 years   $4–$5

When the teen-ager is older he might receive more per month. The exact amount will depend on what expenses the allowance is expected to cover, how much extra income the young person may earn, and the financial resources of the family. (For a sixteen-to-eighteen-year-old, the range could be $25 to $35 a month; for an older boy or girl, $50 to $75.)

Set up a budget and try hard to live within it. Work out a percentage for gas, for entertainment, for snacks, for necessities, for church donations and birthday and Christmas presents too, and stick to it. If you find you simply cannot make ends meet, don't panic. Talk to your parents to see if they can adjust a bit, and try to find a way to earn more money on your own. Don't borrow; once you start that, you'll just find yourself getting deeper and deeper in debt.

Some boys and girls contribute to the family exchequer as soon as they earn money of their own, and others help to pay college tuition and other expenses with scholarships or by taking part-time campus jobs. This is a fine thing to do, but many families do not need or want this sort of help from their children. You'll be mighty popular with your parents, however, if, from time to time, you replenish the soft-drink supply, fill the gas tank when it's not strictly your turn, or add some books or records to the family collection.

## Your Room and Your Clothing

Your first duty in the neatness department is to care for your own room and your clothes. Parents often spend a good deal of time and money in making a youngster's room attractive. When the condition of that room resembles the aftermath of a hurricane, the parents' impression is that their son or daughter doesn't appreciate their efforts. It's just as easy to hang up clothing or put it in the laundry basket the moment it's taken off as it is to do so the next day after your mother's nagging. It takes the same amount of time in either case, and certainly things that can be worn again are in better condition if they've been on a hanger instead of lying in a heap on the floor.

It should be your responsibility, too, to see that your clothes are sent, or taken by you, to the cleaners when necessary. If you have a date for Saturday night, check in advance to see that whatever you're planning to wear is clean and pressed. You can't expect your mother to appreciate hearing—when possibly she's getting ready to go out herself—your desperate shout, "Mother, help! My dress has a spot!" or "Mother, will you iron a shirt for me? I haven't a single clean one in my drawer!"

## Family Rooms

In addition to caring for your own private bailiwick, the responsibility for the community rooms—living room, family room, dining room, and kitchen—should be shared by everyone. I don't mean that you should do the regular housework; that is, of course, your mother's department. I *do* mean that after you and your friends have used these rooms it is up to you to empty ash trays, throw out pop bottles, pick up magazines, cards, and so on from the floor, and in general leave the room ready for the next person who wishes to use it.

Naturally, when your mother tackles an extra-heavy chore such as cleaning out the basement or rearranging the furniture in the recreation room, you should pitch in and help—cheerfully. You'll find if you work hard enough and willingly enough you may even be lucky enough to get paid for it.

Kitchen rules are up to your mother, but she should not be expected to cope with all the dirty dishes or glasses that teen-agers can accumulate. It takes about twenty seconds to rinse out your *own* glass and put it on the drainboard or in the dishwasher, but if one person has to do them all the seconds rapidly add up to hours!

You and your parents should establish definite rules about raiding the refrigerator. While your family may try to keep you supplied with soft drinks and snacks, a gang of teen agers can go through an enormous amount of food, and it's not fair to expect your mother to feed unlimited numbers. Certain shelves, cupboards, drawers should be "family only" and respected as off limits to marauders; otherwise the food your mother had counted on for dinner may well have disappeared into sandwiches at lunchtime.

## TV Sets and Radios

TV sets and radios are usually community property and merit good care from the whole family. Don't leave them blaring when you go out. It wastes the tubes or batteries, as well as being an annoyance to whoever finally turns them off. When there are people resting, or trying to read or work in the house, keep the volume down. Late at night, especially, and early on weekend mornings, turn the sound as low as you possibly can: your parents and younger brothers and sisters and nearby neighbors may need their sleep much more than you do! If you, or one of your friends, is responsible for damaging a set, it is up to you to see that it is fixed, and to pay for, or at least share in, the cost of repairs.

## The Family Car

When you reach legal driving age, and your parents give you permission to get your license, you are assuming an enormous responsibility. A car is an expensive possession, costly both to buy and to maintain. Its operation is potentially dangerous, and therefore subject to many regulations which you must obey. The fact that your mother and father consider you mature enough to have earned the privilege of driving is a real demonstration of their trust in you. Never, never betray that trust.

When you are old enough to use the family car, it is only fair that you pay part of the costs. This means contributing as much as you can to the extra insurance fees that will be charged because of your use of the car. It also means working out an arrangement with your parents about the cost of gas and upkeep. Some families allow their children to use credit cards and to repay them when the chits come in. The amount may be deducted from an allowance or paid in cash from money earned. Others make deals involving car washing in return for X number of gallons of gasoline, etc.

Try to remember that the family car does belong to your parents and they have the first right to it. When you know that you'll need it for a weekend night, ask them well in advance so that they can plan accordingly, or so that, if they need it, you can make other plans for transportation. If you're not continually asking to use the car, they'll be far more agreeable when you really want it. Offer to run errands occasionally, *before* your mother asks you to. You'll pile up lots of credit by taking your little sister to the beach or going—cheerfully—for a forgotten quart of milk.

Most important, never take the car without securing permission. The first time Mom or Dad misses an appointment because you've disappeared with no trace, you might as well turn in your license—and rightfully so.

One reason that parents are sometimes reluctant to allow their teen-agers to use the car is the mess they may find afterward—chewing gum and candy wrappers, dirty socks, combs, books and magazines, all manner of debris on the floor and the seats. If you don't have a trash receptacle in the car (and every family should—you might give one to your dad next Christmas), clean out the car before your parents have a chance to get near it.

Both boys and girls should know the simple mechanics of where oil and hydraulic fluid go into the car, how often the water in the radiator and battery should be checked and how to change a tire. Girls don't have to do the last job very often because a chivalrous man usually stops to help, but it's a very good thing to know when you're stuck on a remote country road.

You should also know all about getting in touch with your insurance company, and what information you should collect when you're involved in an accident. It is only fair to your father for you to be able to give the police and the insurance people all the facts so that he will be able to collect any insurance money that may be due.

If you are arrested for a serious traffic violation—speeding, reckless driving, or any other—don't go crying to your parents for help. Driving is an adult privilege; if you infringe on that privilege you must take the consequences. Parents may help with advice, of course; they may even make you a loan if you are unable to pay a fine. But more than that they cannot do legally, and should not, morally. Therefore, the results of your actions are on your own shoulders. Justify your parents' faith in you by obeying the law scrupulously, and by using caution and good judgment every time you drive a car.

## Borrowing

At one time or another you must have been the victim of a predatory borrower. Jane goes to her drawer to get her navy sweater—and it's not there. Her sister Fran comes home from a date three hours later, wearing it. Tom goes to the rack to get his tennis racquet. It's not there either, and after accusing everyone in the tennis shop of carelessness, or worse, he sees his friend Joe using it on the far court.

You all know what I'm talking about. The article gets returned, but only after time has been wasted looking for it, and tempers have flared. So borrow as little as possible, and *only* with permission. This means from *anyone*—mother, father, brother, sister, or friend. And, when you do, treat the borrowed article with more care than you would if it were your own. If, by some unfortunate chance it is lost or damaged, replace it or have it repaired immediately, and take no argument or "never mind" about it from the owner.

# 3 Your Home Life

A family is a unit but it is made up of individuals. Each of these individuals has his own likes and dislikes, his own talents, his own personality, which may clash violently with the characteristics of other members of his family. You may even actively dislike one or more of your brothers and sisters. Yet, in order to make the home a livable place, a mode of conduct must be worked out among these widely varying personalities.

Although there is no clear-cut solution to this problem, etiquette can help to smooth off the jagged edges. By teaching us to respect the rights and the individualism of each member of the family it can serve to improve the unity of the whole. You, for instance, have a certain relationship with your mother; your sister Jane has quite a different one. Nobody likes everyone else to the same degree—that is something we must simply learn to accept. You *must* learn to respect Jane's right to your mother's affection; you *should* learn to live with Jane's possible preference for your younger sister.

Every member of a family has a right to his own separate life. The ability to allow your parents and your brothers and sisters to lead their private lives is important. Don't, unless asked, involve yourself in their problems. For instance, if you see Mom and Jane having a serious discussion, don't butt in with "What are you two talking about?" Make yourself scarce until they're through, and forget about it. If either one wants to tell you about it she will, but that is her choice, not yours.

The success or failure of family life depends on everyone in the family. If each and every member does not make an active effort to get along with the others, to cooperate and participate, home life becomes just a group of people living under the same roof. It loses all resemblance to a cohesive family unit.

The most obvious way to cooperate is to share—willingly—in the chores. It is up to your parents to decide in what areas they need your assistance, and together you should settle on a fair schedule. It may involve setting the table, washing the dog, polishing the car, or anything else which affects the whole group. Whatever it is, accept your jobs with good grace, and do your full part. No one likes the fellow who is always trying to add his share to someone else's duties. In the interest of fairness, chores should be rotated, so that the monotony of doing the same old thing day after day will be avoided.

Equal in importance to sharing the chores, is willingness to take blame and criticism. If you try to wriggle out of every accusation, true or untrue, you'll find that everyone in the family goes out of his way to put the blame on you. There's nothing wrong in admitting a mistake, but the way in which some people try to deny or justify a trivial fault magnifies it into a crime of the first degree. When you're at fault, admit it. If an apology is in order, make it with sincerity, correct the fault if possible, and avoid a repeat.

The third essential that makes a happier home life for everyone is participation. Enthusiasm for family projects and willingness to enter into them is awfully important. However, let's face it—we all do have moods and times when we just don't feel like taking part in a group activity. When one of these "isolationist" moods hits, your

parents should respect your feelings, and not force you to participate. In return for this respect, it's up to you to let the rest of the
family enjoy what they're doing without you. In other words, don't
be a wet blanket, don't mope, and don't sneer. The best course is
to leave the scene pleasantly. Just say, "Dad, I'd really rather read
for a while," and then go to your room. Read, play records, write
letters, or take a snooze until the mood wears off. Your parents may
be upset to think you don't want to join in, but at least you won't
spoil the fun for the others.

At other times when you really have no particular excuse except
that the activity may not be your idea of the greatest fun, make
yourself join in. Decorating the Christmas tree, helping out at little
sister's or brother's party, planting the garden, building a dog-
house—almost any project can be fun, depending on your attitude.
If you sit on the sidelines, enjoying the results but not entering
into the work, take my word for it you'll diminish not only the
pleasure of the rest of the family, but your own too.

Now here are some suggestions that are more specific, but all of
which are very much tied up with the general thoughts discussed
above.


## Mealtimes

Dinnertime may well be the only hour of the day when your family
is together, so you should help to make it just as pleasant as possible. Don't choose mealtime to bring up the fact that Jimmy owes
you two dollars or Sue broke your favorite record and hasn't replaced it. Nor is it the time to ask for the family car for Saturday
night when you have already been turned down three times. Try to
keep the conversation on subjects interesting to everyone. Even a
good honest difference of opinion can be fun.

Get to meals on time, or at once when you are called.

If you have an appointment at seven, tell your mother well in
advance—not at six forty-five. Offer to fix *yourself* something ahead
of time if it is inconvenient for the rest of the family to eat earlier
than usual.

Come to the table looking neat and clean. If you girls must put
up your hair for a date, cover up with a scarf or turban.

Ask permission in advance when you want to invite a friend for a meal. Your mother may well have to tell you, "Oh dear, I only have four chops," when the prospective guest is already inside the door. By the same token, let your mother know if you're going to be out, so she can put that fourth chop in the freezer.

## The TV Set

If a family has only one TV set, then obviously a priority system should be worked out. Your parents—and not just because they bought the set—undoubtedly have undisputed first choice of programs. With this point conceded, you still must work out an arrangement with your brothers and/or sisters. Age is *not* the criterion—in fact, since little ones are sent to bed earlier, you should occasionally let them have a few extra choices during the early evening hours. Certain days or hours may be allotted to each person, or the agreement may be to allow each one his particular favorite program. Of course, if two favorites come at the same time, you'll have to resort to drawing lots or some such means of settling the issue. It's a sticky problem, but ask your parents to referee, and have them lay down a fair set of rules.

## Dates

*Keep your parents informed of your plans at all times.* That is the most important rule of all about dating. In your younger teen years, you should ask their permission before making a date. Later you may only need to tell them where and when you're going and what you're going to do.

Girls should introduce all new dates to their parents, and bring them in to talk for a few moments. This not only indicates to your mother and father that you are proud of them and want their opinion of your friends, but it lets your new date know that you're not exactly ashamed of him, either.

Don't try to include dates (or friends of the same sex) on every family outing. Your parents sometimes enjoy having a chance to talk to you privately about personal or family matters without benefit of comments from your closest pal.

## Household Help

Domestic help, either part-time or live-in, must be treated with respect and consideration. You may ask, politely, for an occasional favor such as getting a shirt or blouse ironed, but don't add a lot of extra chores to regular duties, and don't ever give *orders* yourself. That is your mother's or father's job, never yours.

## Closed Doors

Everyone needs privacy at times. A closed door requires a knock and a "Come in" before entering, and therefore insures you your privacy. But the privilege of retiring from your family in that way should not be overdone. A closed door whispers, "I've got a secret," and nobody likes being left out of a secret. A locked door is an insult to the rest of your family. It shouts, "I don't trust you," and that attitude is scarcely an asset to family harmony.

# WHEN YOU'RE
# IN PUBLIC

# 4 Restaurant Dining

Going to a restaurant for dinner is certainly one of the greatest ways to start off a date. Most dates, unless they're very special occasions, start after dinner, so when a boy calls a girl and says, "How about going to the Red Horse Inn for dinner tonight?" she knows this is important. She doesn't want to fluff it by looking like Unsophisticated Sally, who has never dined in a restaurant before, and he would undoubtedly like to give the impression that he takes a girl to dinner every other Saturday night. It's not hard for either one to achieve that air of experience, but there are a few things they should learn in advance. Otherwise, they may get into an "After you; no, after you" situation, or they may have the waitress near tears by the confused way in which they order.

When Joan and Jerry arrive at a restaurant in a city, Jerry opens the door, and Joan goes through first. If they drive to a restaurant outside the city, where there is a parking lot, Jerry may let Joan off at the door, and go on alone to park the car. This is especially practical if it's raining or windy, or if there's a rough stone driveway—difficult for a girl to manage in high heels. Joan waits just inside the restaurant door, and they go into the dining room together. Some girls prefer to stay with their dates, but I'd rather spend a moment alone than walk in with my carefully combed hairdo blown to bits.

Once inside, Jerry checks his coat but not Joan's. She may, and should, check an umbrella or packages because they are a nuisance at the table, but she wears her coat to the table and drops the shoulders over the back of her chair when she is seated. Some restaurants won't check a woman's coat at all, but in any case keeping her coat with her will save Jerry an extra quarter in tips. If Joan is wearing gloves, she keeps them on until she sits down, and then she removes them and puts them in a pocket or into her purse. Her hat, if she's wearing one, stays firmly on her head.

If a headwaiter meets them at the entrance (this is obviously a *very* special restaurant), Joan follows him to a table with Jerry bringing up the rear. She is given the choice seat—the one with the best view, or the comfortable banquette against the wall. When they are both to sit on the banquette, Joan waits for the waiter to pull out the table and slides in first. At a regular table, the waiter holds the chair for her, and Jerry sits down after she is settled. He may, but need not if conditions make it awkward, help her off with her coat. If the restaurant is the type where you fend for yourself, Jerry leads the way to a table and pulls out a chair for Joan. If he wants to really chalk up some credits, he may ask her, "Do you want to sit by the window, or shall we take that little table in the corner where we can talk?"

## Would You Care for a Cocktail?

If they're in a state where older teen-agers may order drinks, a waiter will appear almost immediately to ask if they'd like a cocktail. Joan tells Jerry what she would like, and he orders for both of them. If she doesn't want an alcoholic drink, she tells Jerry so, and asks for tomato juice or a soft drink. He'll respect her much more if she is honest and saves him the price of a cocktail, than if she orders something she doesn't want and leaves it untouched on the table.

## Ordering Is Fun!

Jerry asks for the menu if it hasn't been handed to them already, and the fun begins. It's perfectly acceptable for them to discuss the menu or to ask each other about a dish which one of them may not be familiar with. It makes one's mouth water just to talk about the good things on the menu, and besides it will give Joan some idea of the price range that fits Jerry's wallet. It's also quite correct for them to call the waiter over and ask him to describe *zabaglione, gazpacho,* or anything they've never heard of. Once the decisions are made, Joan tells Jerry what she has decided on, and he gives the order to the waiter. If the waiter asks her how she wants her steak cooked, or what sort of salad dressing she prefers, she answers him directly, not relaying her words through Jerry. Joan need not order as many courses as Jerry does, but she certainly shouldn't order more. It just doesn't give that fragile, feminine effect!

MENUS

There are two kinds of menus—*à la carte* and *table d'hôte,* and you should know what each means.

An *à la carte* menu lists each item with a price beside it and the cost of *each* dish you order is added up to make up your total bill. *Table d'hôte* or "complete dinner" has a price beside the main course (often called the entrée), and then lists certain items—first courses, soups, vegetables, salads, and desserts—with no prices. You may choose one item from each of these groups, unless the menu says otherwise, and the cost is included in the price of the entrée. However, beware! There are almost invariably some items listed in these categories which do have prices beside them and, if they do, that amount is charged in addition to that of the main course. Many "complete dinner" menus will say, "Price of entrée includes vegetable, potatoes, and dessert." In this case, the price of anything else, such as soup, salad, or coffee, will be added to your bill.

*Table d'hôte* dinners are usually less expensive than the same items ordered one by one, but remember that you must stay within the limits of what the menu says or the cost of your dinner will skyrocket.

## *Actually Eating*

When the waiter brings bread and butter, and if he brings celery, olives, or other snacks, Joan and Jerry should refrain from diving in as if they were on the verge of starvation. Gorging on those appetizing little tidbits is fun, but it takes the edge off the appetite for the better things to follow.

Table manners are, of course, exactly the same as at home. The piece of silver farthest from the plate is the one used first, unless a special implement such as a little fork is brought in with the shrimp or other first course. Bread should be broken into reasonable-sized (not bite-sized) pieces. If necessary, salad may be cut with a knife. Unless it's a very informal "chicken-in-the-basket" type of restaurant, meat is always cut off the bones, and the bones are not picked up in the fingers. Joan needn't finish every morsel on her plate, but it's apt to insult both the management and Jerry if she sends food back almost untouched.

If either of them orders something which he has never seen before, and neither one knows how it should be eaten, there's no cause for panic. No one else in the restaurant is likely to be paying any attention anyway, so as long as Jerry goes slowly and doesn't make a mess of the table as he's eating the food, and Joan doesn't break into hysterical laughter watching him, the difficulty will pass unnoticed. They can ask the waiter how to manage, but if they don't want to do that, they should just attack it in the neatest way they can invent.

## Reluctantly Leaving

After finishing the fabulous meal, Joan and Jerry have to break the spell and get organized to leave. Jerry asks for the check, and while he is going over it mentally—not with a pencil and slide rule—Joan may touch up her lipstick or add a little powder right there. However, she may *not* comb her hair or go in for extensive repairs to her make-up. For that she must say, "Excuse me, Jerry. I'll be right back," and head for the ladies' room. If she doesn't see the sign anywhere, Joan need not hesitate to ask the nearest waiter where it is—he is asked the same question at least a dozen times a night. If there is an attendant, there will also be a little dish left in an obvious spot, and Joan is expected to leave a quarter.

When Joan gets back to the table, and the waiter returns with the change, Jerry picks it up and leaves the tip (fifteen percent is still the accepted tip everywhere but in the most luxurious restaurants. To figure it quickly, take ten percent of the check and add half of that amount). He helps Joan into her coat, and then holds her chair or pulls the table away so that she can get up easily. They both make certain that they haven't left gloves, cigarettes, or anything else; thank the waiter if he is nearby; and leave. If the check says, "Please Pay Cashier," Jerry would leave the correct amount for the tip, and they would leave together, stopping at the cashier's desk to pay the check. If he did not have the correct change for the tip, he would return to leave it on the table after getting change from the cashier. On the way out they retrieve Jerry's coat from the checkroom, and he deposits a quarter in the plate.

## Special Situations

Joan and Jerry's dinner, as described above, was a very easy and pleasant one to cope with—nothing troublesome or out of the ordinary happened at all. And this is the way dining out generally is. However, all sorts of complications can arise, and you ought to be aware of them in advance. If you know how to handle an unusual situation, every dinner, no matter what occurs, can go as smoothly as Joan and Jerry's.

### THE POLITE PROTECTOR

There are unfortunate occasions when something *does* go wrong. You find a button in your soup or lipstick on the glass the waiter is about to fill, or your rare steak arrives looking like shoe leather. It's the man's job to complain, so if the girl has a problem she lets him take care of it. She stays out of the discussion, and he handles it firmly but inconspicuously. He calls the waiter, asks for another cup of soup or a fresh glass, or explains that he ordered the steak rare and it's cooked to a fare-thee-well. If the waiter doesn't co-operate, he catches the headwaiter's eye and explains the situation to him. You may reduce the amount of your tip or leave none at all if the waiter has been really rude, and don't go back to that restaurant. But don't ruin the evening by working yourself and, incidentally, your date into a state of nervous collapse.

### HI, HELLO, AND MOVE ALONG

If you see a group of friends at a nearby table when you arrive, stop and greet them with a "Hi, we didn't know you were coming here tonight," or some such remark, and move on. When you stop to chat, the boys at the table should all stand, so you're cluttering up the passageway for waiters and other customers. If their table is off to one side, just wave; or the first group to leave might stop at the other's table for a brief "Hello."

SUGGESTIONS FOR SMOKERS

If you're going to smoke, try to remember to have enough cigarettes with you. In an expensive restaurant, the price of a pack bought from the cigarette girl is usually exorbitant. In any case, it's a nuisance for a man to have to hunt for a vending machine, and it's an extra expense if he has to tip the waiter to do it for him.

When there is no ash tray on the table, Jerry should ask for one. It is inexcusable to put out cigarettes or drop ashes on the edge of a plate, in your saucer, or on the floor.

If one member of a couple smokes and the other doesn't, the smoker must be careful that the smoke from a cigarette left in an ash tray doesn't drift directly into his companion's face. And don't exhale the smoke right at your date. In a nutshell, if you must smoke, be thoughtful. That's all!

WHEN THERE'S DANCING

When you go to a place where there is dance music, you may get up to dance after you order, while waiting for your meal. Keep an eye on the table, however, so that your soup or meat won't get cold. If the music is so good you can't resist it, dance between courses too, but save a little strength—after dinner you can dance to your heart's content.

A lot of girls wonder what to do about their purses when they get up to dance. Unless you're in a restaurant where you know the clientele is reliable, it's best to leave your purse on the chair seat and push the chair well under the table. It's just too easy for someone to pick up anything left on top of the table and disappear before you can bat an eye. Of course you can carry a small purse in your left hand if you're doing ballroom-type dancing, but it's pretty hard to hold on to *anything* when you're doing the newest dances.

TIPPING HEADWAITERS

A young man is not expected to tip the headwaiter for simply leading him and his date to a table. He is expected to tip if the headwaiter has gone to some trouble to put tables together to accommodate a group, has seen to it that an overdone steak was quickly replaced by a rare one, or has performed any service that could be considered special. If either a boy or a girl is entertaining a group at a restaurant, then the headwaiter who takes care of the party is given a tip.

The tip for arranging a table in a crowded restaurant is usually one or two dollars. The size of the tip when you give a party depends entirely on the size of the group and the amount of service the headwaiter performs. It could be anything from five dollars to much, much more.

DUTCH TREAT DILEMMAS

The only problem—and it's a real one—involved in a group's going Dutch arises when it's time to pay the bill. Far and away the best method to solve this is to ask, when you order, for separate checks. If you forget to do that, or if the waiter objects to the extra work of making individual checks, there are two other outs. You can appoint one person to be banker and have each member give him the same amount, the total of which will more than cover the bill. He then pays it, leaves the tip, and divides and returns the remainder evenly. Or, if the banker has enough cash, he may pay the check and tip, and then collect an even amount from each person to pay him back. The one thing to avoid is that confusing and ridiculous situation where each member of the party tries to add up his or her share and argues about whose dinner cost fifteen cents more, and so on. The waiter goes crazy, the other patrons think you're too juvenile to be out without your parents, and your own party ends up in a battle royal.

## Dining in Foreign Restaurants

There comes a time when even the most ardent fan gets sick of the local hamburger drive-in or steak house, and wants to try something a little different. Nothing is more fun than trying foreign foods, but it does present some problems when you don't understand the menus. I don't expect you to sit down and memorize the following lists, but I think you'll enjoy your first trips to foreign restaurants more if you know just a few things to look for. If nothing else, you'll impress your date if you can say, with authority, that you would like *coq au vin* for your entrée or *zabaglione* for dessert.

Never be afraid to ask for translations—everyone does. The waiter or headwaiter will be delighted to tell you what is in various dishes, and often will recommend those which he thinks are best and that you would enjoy the most. Do try some of the unfamiliar dishes; after all, that's why you left the hamburger palace!

Let's talk about French restaurants first, because French cooking has the generally well-deserved reputation for being the best. The very fancy and better-known French restaurants are extremely expensive, but a young person with limited funds can find many tiny ones tucked away off the main street in every city, and they usually serve superb food at very reasonable prices. In these small places, the menus are almost always in French—and with no translations. If you and your date plan to explore any of these spots, it would be well to spend a little time learning the meaning and pronunciation of some of the words you will surely find on their menus.

As to beverages, if you are of wine-drinking age and taste, you will find that the *vin ordinaire*—the ordinary wine of the restaurant—is cheap and good. It can be ordered by the glass, so you don't have to buy more than you want.

To start your meal, choose from among the following:

| MENU LISTING | WHAT IT IS | HOW TO PRONOUNCE IT (ROUGHLY) |
|---|---|---|

### HORS-D'OEUVRE—APPETIZERS OR FIRST COURSE

| | | |
|---|---|---|
| *Pâté* | Paste of meat, usually liver, and seasonings | |
| *Coquilles Saint-Jacques* | Scallops in a cream sauce served in a shell | |
| *Escargots* | Snails cooked in strong garlic butter | |
| *Moules* | Mussels | |

You may prefer soup to hors-d'oeuvres, and if you do not see *ou* (or) between the two, both are included in the *table d'hôte* or complete dinner.

| MENU LISTING | WHAT IT IS | HOW TO PRONOUNCE IT (ROUGHLY) |
|---|---|---|

## SOUPES, POTAGES—SOUPS

| | | |
|---|---|---|
| *Bisque* | A cream soup made from shellfish | |
| *Bouillabaisse* | Fish soup—almost a stew, served as a main course | |
| *Soupe* or *potage du jour* | Special soup of the day | |
| *Vichyssoise* | Cold potato soup | |

## MISCELLANEOUS

When you're on a lunch rather than a dinner date, you may prefer something light, like eggs or a cheese soufflé. If omelets of various types are listed, ask the waiter to translate. An *omelette fines herbes*—with several herbs—is always delicious.

| | | |
|---|---|---|
| *Oeufs* | Eggs | |
| *Brouillés* | Scrambled | |
| *En cocotte* | Shirred | |
| *Fromage* | Cheese | |

## POISSONS—FISH

| | | |
|---|---|---|
| *Écrevisse* | Crayfish — a delicious shellfish a little larger than a shrimp | |
| *Filet of sole* | Boned slice of the fish | |
| *Langouste, homard* | Lobster | |
| *Truite* | Trout | |

Grilling—broiling over open flame—is not a feature of French cooking, and the best fish dishes are cooked in a sauce. Choose from the following methods of preparation, or ask your waiter to explain others.

| | | |
|---|---|---|
| *Bonne femme* | With white wine and mushrooms | |
| *Meunière* | With butter sauce | |
| *Sauté* | Fried | |

Find your favorite meats among the following, and then look below for a way of preparation that sounds good to you.

| MENU LISTING | WHAT IT IS | HOW TO PRONOUNCE IT (ROUGHLY) |
|---|---|---|
| **VIANDES—MEATS** | | |
| *Agneau* or *Mouton* | Lamb or mutton | |
| *Gigot* or *épaule* | Leg or shoulder | |
| *Côtes* | Chops | |
| *Boeuf* | Beef | |
| *Châteaubriand* | Center cut of filet | |
| *Entrecôte* | Rib, Delmonico or shell steak | |
| *Tournedos* | Individual slices of filet | |
| *Jambon* | Ham | |
| *Porc* | Pork | |
| *Veau* | Veal | |
| *Côtelettes* | Cutlets | |
| *Escalopes* | Very thin cutlets, scaloppine | |

### VARIETY MEATS

The following meats are delicious, but it takes a little courage to try some of them. You'll be well rewarded if you have a sophisticated palate, but you should know the names in any case.

| | | |
|---|---|---|
| *Cervelles* | Brains | |
| *Foie* | Liver | |
| *Langue* | Tongue | |
| *Ris de veau* | Sweetbreads | |
| *Rognons* | Kidneys | |
| *Saucisse, saucisson* | Sausage | |

There are a great many methods of preparing meat. If you don't want to go too far in experimenting, choose a dish described as:

| MENU LISTING | WHAT IT IS | HOW TO PRONOUNCE IT (ROUGHLY) |
|---|---|---|
| *Bonne femme* | Roasted with onions, potatoes, and brown sauce in a casserole | |
| *Bourguignon* | In red wine | |
| *En brochette* | On a skewer | |

Very often a dish followed by the phrase *maître d'hôtel* or the name of the restaurant is worth trying because it means it's a specialty of the house. If you're not willing to take a chance, ask first for a description.

## POULTRY

| | |
|---|---|
| *Canard, caneton* | Duck |
| *Faisan* | Pheasant |
| *Poulet, coq* | Chicken |

The methods of preparing poultry are similar to those for meat, but in this case *grillé* (grilled) is usually a safe, if uninspired choice. The most common choice is:

| | |
|---|---|
| *Coq au vin* | Cooked in red wine with onions and mushrooms |

You may find the words *ragoût* meaning stew, or *sauté* meaning fried, with any kind of meat.

All vegetables may be *au beurre*—with butter. They also may be *braisé*—braised—or in sauce.

## LÉGUMES—VEGETABLES

| | |
|---|---|
| *Artichauts* | Artichokes |
| *Asperges* | Asparagus |
| *Aubergine* | Eggplant |
| *Champignons* | Mushrooms |
| *Chou-fleur* | Cauliflower |
| *Épinard* | Spinach |
| *Haricots verts* | Green beans |

| MENU LISTING | WHAT IT IS | HOW TO PRONOUNCE IT (ROUGHLY) |
|---|---|---|
| *Petits pois* | Peas (extra small) | |
| *Pommes de terre* | Potatoes | |
| *Ratatouille* | Mixture of eggplant, onion and zucchini | |
| *Pilaf* | Rice sautéed with various seasonings | |

Choose your favorite sauce from the list below and watch for them on the menu.

| | | |
|---|---|---|
| *Béarnaise* | Hollandaise with herbs | |
| *Bourguignon, bordelaise* | Red wine sauce | |
| *Gratiné, au gratin* | Topped with cheese, or in cheese sauce | |
| *Provençal* | With tomatoes, garlic and seasoning | |

French desserts are rich and delicious. The following are the most often served, but you're pretty sure to like anything you order.

## ENTREMETS—DESSERTS

| | | |
|---|---|---|
| *Baba au rhum* | Pastry covered with rum syrup | |
| *Crêpes Suzette* | Thin pancakes covered with orange butter, liqueur sauce, served flaming | |
| *Flan* | Custard | |
| *Gâteau* | Cake | |
| *Glace* | Ice Cream | |
| *Mousse* | A fluffy molded dessert, often chocolate | |
| *Pâtisserie* | Pastry | |

| MENU LISTING | WHAT IT IS | HOW TO PRONOUNCE IT (ROUGHLY) |
|---|---|---|
| *Pot de crème* | Rich custard, usually chocolate | |
| *Tarte* | Tart or pie | |

## FRUITS

| | | |
|---|---|---|
| *Ananas* | Pineapple | |
| *Fraises* | Strawberries | |
| *Framboises* | Raspberries | |
| *Pêches* | Peaches | |
| *Poires* | Pears | |
| *Pommes* | Apples | |

Italian restaurants offer the heartiest meals of any at very low prices, if you stick to the *pasta* and specialties. While Italian restaurants may have excellent steaks or roast beef, the more unusual dishes are the stuffed peppers, eggplant parmigiana or the delicious stuffed macaroni and other pasta dishes. Listed below are some of the best Italian dishes. Choose from among them and you'll have a fabulous meal.

## FIRST COURSES

| | | |
|---|---|---|
| *Antipasto* | Mixed hors-d'oeuvre (best when served on a tray from which you can choose) | |
| *Gamberi* | Crayfish | |
| *Pesce* | Fish | |
| *Prosciutto* | Dry-cured raw ham, sliced thin and often served with melon | |
| *Scampi* | Shrimp, cooked with garlic | |

## ZUPPA—SOUP

| | |
|---|---|
| *Brodo* | Broth |
| *Stracciatella inbrodo* | Consommé |
| *Minestrone* | Rich vegetable soup |

## PASTA

Name covering all products such as noodles, spaghetti, macaroni, and the dough they are made from

| | |
|---|---|
| *Cannelloni* | Large rolls of pasta stuffed with meat, tomatoes, cheese, etc. |
| *Fettuccine* | Noodles, usually served with butter and cheese |
| *Gnocchi* | Dumplings made often of a potato flour |
| *Linguine* | Very narrow noodles |
| *Lasagne* | Layers of pasta, cheese, and meat baked in tomato sauce |
| *Manicotti* | Stuffed pasta tubes with a sauce |
| *Spaghettini* | Thin spaghetti |

Linguine, spaghetti and spaghettini are all served with various sauces. The most popular are:

| | |
|---|---|
| *Bolognese* | Meat sauce |
| *Milanese* | Usually cooked with rice, or with butter and cheese |
| *Marinara* | Tomato and garlic sauce |
| *Salsiccia* | Sausage sauce |
| *Vongole* | Clam sauce |

| MENU LISTING | WHAT IT IS | HOW TO PRONOUNCE IT (ROUGHLY) |
|---|---|---|

## CARNI—MEATS

| | |
|---|---|
| *Fegato* | Liver |
| *Pollo* | Chicken |
| *Salsiccia* | Sausage |
| *Saltimbocca* | Ham and veal, some-times with cheese |
| *Vitello* | Veal |
| *Costoletta* | Cutlet |
| *Scaloppine* | Very thin cutlet |

### Meats are most commonly prepared in the following ways:

| | |
|---|---|
| *Alla cacciatora* | In wine and tomato sauce |
| *Formaggio* | With cheese |
| *Marsala* | In a wine sauce |
| *Parmigiana* | With Parmesan cheese |
| *Piccata* | With lemon and butter |

## ERBA OR LEGUMI—VEGETABLES

| | |
|---|---|
| *Carciofii* | Artichokes |
| *Fagioli* | Beans |
| *Insalata* | Salad |
| *Peperoni* | Peppers |
| *Pomidori* | Tomatoes |
| *Riso* | Rice |
| *Risotto* | Rice dish with meat, cheese, or other ingre-dients |

## DOLCI—DESSERTS

| | |
|---|---|
| *Gelati* | Ice cream |
| *Spumoni* | Ice cream with candied fruit and nuts, or a brick of ice cream with three flavors |

| MENU LISTING | WHAT IT IS | HOW TO PRONOUNCE IT (ROUGHLY) |
|---|---|---|
| *Torta* | Tart, pie, cake | |
| *Tortoni* | Wine-flavored vanilla ice cream with a topping of macaroon crumbs | |
| *Zabaglione* | Wine-flavored custard | |

Mexican restaurants are great if you like your food "hot"—in the spicy sense. Most people who live in the South or Far West are familiar with these dishes, but for those who come from other parts of the country the following specialties are among the best known and will be found on almost every Mexican menu:

| | | |
|---|---|---|
| *Chile con carne* | Meat in a hot chili sauce served with beans | |
| *Enchiladas* | Tortillas with sausage, cheese, and hot sauce | |
| *Frijoles* | Beans (red or kidney) | Free-*hole*-ehs |
| *Guacamole* | Mashed, flavored avocado—salad or hors-d'oeuvre | |
| *Tacos* | Dough folded around meat filling, and fried crisp | *Tock*-os |
| *Tortillas* | Semi-crisp round of cornmeal dough, usually rolled around a filling of meat and sauce | Tore-*tea*-yas |

Spanish food is often mistakenly assumed to be similar to Mexican, but this is not the case. It is not "hot" and it features rice and seafood rather than various doughs. Here are a few specialties:

| | | |
|---|---|---|
| *Arroz con pollo* | Chicken and rice cooked together | a-*ros* cone *pole*-yo |
| *Gazpacho* | Cold vegetable soup | |

| MENU LISTING | WHAT IT IS | HOW TO PRONOUNCE IT (ROUGHLY) |
|---|---|---|
| Paella | The most famous dish of southern Spain—rice cooked with chicken, veal, and/or a variety of shellfish | pie-*el*-ya |
| Seviche | An hors-d'oeuvre of fish —"cooked" by soaking in lemon or lime juice | |

I don't know of anything more delicious than good Chinese food. It has the advantage of not being heavy or too filling, and Chinese restaurants are often less expensive than almost any others.

Fortunately, the menus in most of them not only translate the names of the dishes but usually also describe them. The names, however, are so complicated and variable that I wouldn't attempt to list them. Instead I will make some suggestions as to what to look for in each course.

The soups are clear rather than thick, and won ton, one of the most popular, has dumplings and pieces of meat in it.

For a first course, spareribs with sweet and sour sauce are delicious. So are egg rolls—light dumplings filled with shrimp, chicken, or meat and vegetables. These names generally appear in English on the menu. Many Chinese restaurants serve Cantonese-style food, and in these the most familiar main course will be *chow mein*—a mixture of chicken, meat, lobster, or shrimp served with fried noodles. It is delicious, but can be bought canned or frozen, so why not try something new when you have the chance?

There are also many Chinese restaurants that feature Northern Chinese cooking—Mandarin or Shanghai. These offer steamed fish in ginger sauce, duckling prepared in several types of sauces, sweet-and-sour soups, and other unusual dishes.

Because of the translation difficulties with their menus, waiters in Chinese restaurants, more than in any others, are ready and willing to help you make a choice. In many restaurants they will bring small servings of several dishes so that everyone in your group can take and try a little of each. Crisp water chestnuts, snow peas (in the pod), bamboo shoots, and bean sprouts—all served with many dishes—are among the best-tasting vegetables in the world.

Don't refuse the marvelous tea that is invariably served. For some reason, nothing else goes as well with Chinese food as their special tea. And for dessert, the famous fortune cookies are fun to open; you can find out what the future holds!

Restaurants serving foods that are specialties of many other foreign countries are equally interesting, and each provides at least some fascinating dishes. Japanese restaurants are similar to Chinese restaurants in their preparation of crisp vegetables. In addition, they often feature dishes prepared in a chafing dish at your own table. There is never any need to be nervous or shy about eating in a foreign restaurant. Remember, the more exotic the food, the more accustomed the waiters are to assisting you.

# 5 At the Theater, Movies, and Sports Events

Their dinner having been a smashing success, Jerry invites Joan to the theater the following week. He gets the tickets in advance and picks Joan up in plenty of time to arrive ten minutes or so before curtain time. If he's taking her to dinner first, they should allow an extra fifteen minutes for unexpected delays.

## GETTING TO THEIR SEATS

Jerry guides Joan ahead of him as he gives both tickets to the man at the door and waits for the return of the stubs. The man will direct them to the proper aisle, and an usher (usually a woman) will meet them there, show them to their seats, and hand each of them a playbill. If the ushers are very busy, Jerry and Joan start down the aisle themselves, Jerry leading the way. Should Jerry find someone sitting in what he believes to be their seats, he checks his tickets and quietly and politely tells the poacher: "I believe you're sitting in our seats." If this doesn't dislodge the intruder—or should Jerry have any difficulty finding his seats—he immediately returns to the aisle and gives his tickets to an usher. Joan stands out of the way—next to an empty seat or in the aisle—until the problem is solved.

If it were Joan who had the tickets and invited Jerry to go with her, she would give them to him in advance. If the tickets were held for them at the box office, or if Jerry were buying them at the theater, he would stand in line and Joan would wait out of the flow of traffic in the crowded lobby. A word of warning, however. If it's a new play, a popular one, or a limited engagement, his chances of getting tickets at the last minute are slim. If there is any doubt about it, it is far safer to order them ahead of time.

When they reach their row, Joan goes in first. If they're double dating, one boy may go in first, then his date, then the other girl, and the second boy last. Girls often like this arrangement because they can talk between acts, but for this very reason boys may prefer to alternate, sending one girl in first. Either system is correct.

If, in spite of all their planning, Jerry and Joan arrive after the curtain has gone up, they wait at the back of the theater until the end of the first scene or until an usher indicates that she will show them quietly to their places. Or, if it's a musical, they may quietly slip into the row during the applause following a song and dance number.

COATS AND HATS

Jerry may check his coat if he wishes, but many men prefer not to because of the delay in retrieving it when the show is over. This poses the problem of what to do with it during the performance. It can be folded up and put under the seat if it's made of a material that won't show a little dirt, or it can be folded and held in the lap. The same applies to a man's hat—without folding, of course! Joan has no problem; Jerry helps her slip out of her coat and drapes it over the back of the seat, and she may leave it there when she goes to the lobby during intermissions. If Joan is wearing a hat that might conceivably block one inch of stage for the person behind her, she must remove it. She should do so before she is asked, but certainly at once when it is called to her attention.

### INTERMISSION

Most people like to get up and walk around during intermission, if only to stretch their legs. But sometimes they don't, and if Joan and Jerry have decided to go out they simply say, "Excuse me," and wait for the others to stand and let them pass. They edge by, facing the stage, and Joan makes sure that her handbag doesn't swing against the heads of the people in the row in front. Getting back to their seats, they go through the same procedure, saying as they pass, "Thank you; I'm sorry to bother you." If they decide to remain in their places, they should stand and push their seats back to let people by. Nothing is more awkward than having to climb over someone who remains planted in his seat with knees drawn to one side—*supposedly* out of the way!

### THEATER CLOTHES

Jerry will want to look his best when he goes to the theater, so he'll probably wear a suit; but, in any event, he must wear a jacket and tie.

Joan may wear anything from an afternoon dress to a dinner dress. The happy medium is a cocktail dress or suit, and she'll feel comfortable and smart in either one. If she's a working girl and has to meet Jerry before she has an opportunity to change, she'd be smart to carry some extra jewelry and fresh gloves in her purse to perk up her daytime clothes.

### "DO UNTO OTHERS"

Presuming that you're enjoying the play yourself, you'll have an even better time if the people around you are enjoying it too. I'm sure you've been seated behind or near people who:

Can't sit still. They keep switching from one side to the other and, as a result, a whole line of people behind them keep trying to outguess them, driving each other crazy.

Talk during the performance. They loudly ask, "What did she say? I didn't hear it." Or they explain the jokes to their knuckle-headed dates all during the show. Unfortunately, there isn't much you can do about it, except ask them politely to keep their voices down.

If you want to smoke during the intermission, wait until you reach the outer lobby. Lighting cigarettes inside the theater is usually against fire regulations and it adds to the work of the ushers and doormen who are responsible for seeing these rules are obeyed.

## Movies

Movie manners are much more lenient than theater manners, but the basics are similar. No one should behave in such a way as to interfere with the rest of the audience's enjoyment. The same rules hold true about wearing hats, making noise, and climbing over people. Generally, paper wrappings should be removed from candy and snacks before you go in. If that's impossible, as in the case of popcorn or nuts, try not to rattle the paper. You know how you feel when you hear that constant crackle in the row behind you. If you chew gum, please do so with your mouth closed, and don't stick the leftover wad under your seat or drop it on the floor. Wrap it in a piece of paper or tissue, and keep it until you find a trash can.

At the movies in the country or the suburbs, you can wear almost anything as long as it's reasonably neat, clean, and modest, but in the city a girl looks much better in a dress or skirt than she does in slacks or shorts.

The need for considering others has to be stressed so far as movies are concerned, because young people often go in groups and this does lead to noise. Remember that other people in the movie house paid to be there too, and they have a right to hear the sound track. But they can't if a group is giggling, making loud remarks, and wandering back and forth to the refreshment stand in a steady stream. Also, remember that two heads together are twice as hard

to see around as one. Save your love-making for another, more private, time. It's in poor taste in public, especially when it actually bothers your neighbors.

## Sports Events

### CLOTHES FOR OUTDOOR AND INDOOR GAMES

The most important thing about clothing for football games in the more northerly parts of the country is that it keeps you warm. Slacks and boots, fur coats, ski parkas—you can wear anything and everything that keeps you from freezing. It's a good idea to take along a thermos of hot soup or coffee, too. In the warmer climates, comfortable sports clothes of a less bizarre nature are worn.

However, baseball spectators usually wear more informal clothes than football fans. In the bleachers and regular stands, all sorts of informal outfits, including slacks and shorts, are worn; but a girl sitting in a private box should wear a skirt.

At indoor sports arenas, the spectators in the better seats dress up considerably more than those in the upper balconies. Dresses and suits or skirts and sweaters are worn by the girls, and jackets and ties by the men. Events such as horse or dog shows require a dressier appearance than do basketball or hockey games.

ENJOY THE GAME!

The main thing you want to do as a spectator at any sport is to enjoy yourself, and, happily, there are few restrictions to keep you from doing so. But there are some guidelines that will help you to have the best possible time, and they will add to the fun of everyone around you.

1. Arrive on time so that you won't disturb the early birds by climbing over them to reach your seats or block their view of the first exciting play as you pass in front of them.
2. There's nothing wrong with shouting and cheering all you want for your team and your favorite player, as long as you don't make nasty cracks about the other team. It's unsporting, and you may find yourself the target of vicious remarks from your neighbors.
3. When you jump up—and you will—in moments of crisis, you'll rapidly discover the people behind you want to see too. Unless you sit down as soon as the crisis is over, you'll be deluged with furious shouts of "Down in front!"
4. If you smoke be careful not to jab or brush against anyone with your cigarette. Try to hold it so that smoke doesn't keep drifting into your neighbor's face.
5. If you've ever been caught in a hurrying, shoving mob, you'll know why they say, "When the game is over, *walk, don't run* to the nearest exit." Most important, don't shove. Walk *with* the crowd, not *through* it, to the gate.

# YOUR PERSONAL
# APPEARANCE

# 6 Especially for the Girls

Your appearance is the most immediate and important factor in creating the impression you wish to make. If you want to cause an instant sensation, you'll know how to do it without any help from me. Tight sweaters, low-cut necklines, heavy make-up will turn heads all right, but I don't believe that is the sort of attention you really want. I'm sure most of you basically want to be thought of as chic and well dressed. To achieve that takes a lot of effort and thought; it doesn't just happen. Of course, the more it *looks* as if it has come about naturally, the more successful you've been.

## Cleanliness and Neatness

There are two requirements which are undeniably essential to an attractive appearance—cleanliness and neatness. Personal hygiene—keeping yourself clean and fresh—is too obvious a necessity to waste words on. It's enough to say that daily baths or showers, strict adherence to your dentist's recommendations, and regular breaks to comb your hair and repair your make-up should be a part of everyone's daily routine.

Neatness goes hand in hand with cleanliness, and one is rarely found without the other. The girl who takes the trouble to keep her hair clean and neat, and her hands and nails groomed, usually cares enough about her appearance to see that her clothes are immaculate too. They are pressed and laundered or cleaned frequently.

Long before a stranger notices the style of your dress, he is struck by the general impression you create. Are you sloppy and grubby, or are you trim and clean? It doesn't matter *what* you wear—levis, skirt and sweater, or an evening gown—as long as it fits you, is right for the occasion, and is clean and neat.

## *Hair Care*

It is a medical fact that a teen-ager's hair is oilier than an adult's. This means more time and attention if you want it to look its best. Two, or even three, washings a week and rinsing with a good hair conditioner are often necessary. This necessity for frequent shampoos suggests that a very simple hairdo, requiring little setting, would be ideal. If you can wear your hair long and straight, or drawn back smoothly, you're one of the lucky ones. But if your hair just won't fall the right way, or has too much curl in it to lie flat, there's nothing to do but spend a large part of your time with your hair rolled up in curlers. Since this is hardly the way you'd want to be seen by your boy friend, or anyone else, try to use those hours for study, reading, or letter writing—anything that can be done in your room. If you are a lucky stoic and can sleep on curlers, great! But otherwise, remember that even doting parents can be disenchanted by the sight of that roller helmet. If you must come to a meal before your hair is dry, cover up with a turban, a scarf, or a silly curler cover.

Your own natural hair color is probably the most becoming to you, but if you want to bring out the high lights or accentuate the blondness or darkness with a rinse, do it with care and restraint. For one thing, constant coloring will damage your hair in time. Choose your dye or tint carefully; some are available that contain a hair conditioner. And keep the color very close to your natural shade. The difference in the color at the roots as your hair grows out will be less noticeable, and your hair will still match your complexion.

As to style, the first and most important thing to consider is, "Is it becoming to *me?*" Of course, everyone tries the newest look, but if the current fad doesn't do anything for you, find a style that isn't too extreme in any direction and wait it out. Hair styles change almost as fast as the length of your skirts.

In general, the simplest hairdo is the most becoming. The quality of a young person's hair—its sheen and softness—can be completely destroyed by too much teasing and ratting. Naturalness goes best with a young face.

## Hand Care

There are only a few things to be said about hands and nails, but they are awfully important. To begin with, start using a good lubricating hand cream when you're really young. Your skin, when you're fourteen, looks as if it would never have a wrinkle, and if it gets regular care from then on it won't. But ignore the sunburn, the chapping, and the roughness, and all of a sudden those wrinkles are there—and it's too late to do much about them!

The condition of your nails gives away a lot of secrets about your personality. For instance, if they're chewed to the nub, chances are you're a nervous person, or not very sure of yourself—something you don't want to advertise. Do your level best to stop that nibbling; besides ruining the looks of your hands, it's not very attractive to watch.

While nails bitten off at the quick are positively barbaric, so are long cat claws. Besides, they're terribly impractical if you're anything but a lounge lizard. They're bound to break if you go out for sports, and nothing's worse looking than one short, one long, or jagged stumps.

Nail polish tends to make some people's nails brittle, but if it doesn't bother yours, choose a lightish shade that goes well with your complexion and clothes: orange for redheads and brunettes, pink for blondes, and one of the lustrous shades to go with your evening clothes. *Most* important of all, when the polish starts to chip, take it off with remover and start over again. The only sight worse than half-on, half-off polish is someone sitting in a public spot, chipping the remainder off bit by bit.

## Make-up

Make-up is designed to *enhance* your looks—not to disguise them! Nothing spoils a young girl's appearance more effectively than make-up applied with a trowel. It is a real art to put make-up on correctly, and it is well worth the effort. Study the tips in the fashion magazines, learn from friends who apply their make-up well, or consult an expert in a beauty salon.

You should be allowed to wear make-up at about the same age you start to go to mixed parties, or to date—at thirteen or fourteen. During the first few years you should not wear make-up to school, or during the daytime, unless you are attending a wedding or some other special event. Begin with a pale shade of lipstick and face powder. Try different tones to see which go well with your complexion. If you tend to wear browns and greens, lipstick with an orange tinge is more becoming; if you lean toward blues or reds, the clear pinks are a better choice.

Older girls often want to wear make-up to school, and there is no reason not to as long as it is worn in moderation. Stick to lipstick and powder during school hours, and for games and outdoor activities. For a day of shopping or theatergoing in the city, add a delicate line to your eyelids, and a touch of mascara if you need it.

For special evening occasions, use a good powder base, which will cover up any flaws in your complexion and will hold the powder you apply on top of it. A small amount of blue or gray eye shadow helps to enlarge and emphasize your eyes. Don't go in for startling colors and luminous make-up—it only works if you're on the stage. If your eyebrows are pale, darken them slightly with an eyebrow pencil, and use a delicate touch to line your eyes and apply mascara. The whole secret is subtlety. A heavy hand with the make-up turns you into a caricature; a light one adds immeasurably to your appearance.

The same rule applies to perfume. It is out of place in school or outdoors, but in the evening a light scent, sparingly used, is very appealing.

## The Girl with a Figure Problem

Girls with figure problems can do a lot to help themselves. If you've lost the battle of the bulge, avoid large prints, broad stripes (especially horizontal ones), and bulky materials. Your clothes shouldn't be tight, but neither should they be baggy or gathered at the waist. The A-line is more flattering than either a straight one or a dirndl. Clothes should be simple—tailored rather than frilly—and solid colors, especially black and navy blue, are the most slimming. If your legs are heavy, don't call attention to them by wearing short, short skirts. "Stretch" bathing suits or bikinis will just push the bulges out, above and below. It's painful to hear, but you should give up shorts and slacks until you've lost those twenty pounds.

Thin girls have fewer problems than their opposites, but there are some things worth remembering. High collars, and turtlenecks are usually becoming—they hide bony shoulders and shorten long necklines. Nubbly materials are especially good for a slim figure, and, of course, these gals can wear slacks, shorts, and straight skirts as if they had been designed especially for them.

If you are very tall, choose clothes with a waistline or a division of some sort in the middle. A wide belt or a skirt and top of contrasting colors will break the long look. Low heels are in style now, but even when they're not there are shops which feature special shoes to reduce your inches without sacrificing smartness. Above all, and this is vital to your appearance, *don't slump!* If you're uncomfortable with a shorter man, it's better not to go out with him, rather than spend the evening hunched over like an inchworm. Your whole appearance can be undone if you go around apologizing for your height. Wear it proudly. Let people say admiringly, "That's a lot of woman!"

The five-foot-two-and-under picks just the opposite sort of clothes. A long, uninterrupted line, princess or sheath, does the most to add inches. High heels obviously help if you can walk gracefully in them, and a hairdo with a little fullness on top can stretch you upward a bit. Avoid overpowering clothes—you don't have the height to carry them off.

# 7 Dressing for the Occasion

Is it becoming? Is it appropriate? These are the two questions every girl must ask herself *first,* before she thinks of color, style, or any other quality in her clothes.

## Is It Becoming?

I try to avoid talking about styles; they change too rapidly, and I don't want to start an argument about what is good-looking and what isn't.

I do want to talk, however, about how to decide what looks best on *you*. Naturally, you're not going to wear dresses to your calves if the current fad finds hems halfway up your thighs, nor will you appear in a full, flowing chiffon if a slim sheath is the rage. But don't be just a follower all the time; a little originality makes you stand out from the crowd. If everyone else is wearing basic black to the party, choose a bright color or a print. If hats look well on you, wear one, even though the other girls have nothing on their heads but a bow. With a little intelligent planning, you can accentuate your best features and hide and disguise any bad ones. Any teen-ager who slips into a size ten or twelve without alterations can wear almost any style she wants, and she'll look wonderful in it, but don't despair if you're not one of the lucky ones. Far more important than wearing the same size as most of your friends is being sure that the size you choose is right for you. Buy from the stores which feature styles which are most becoming to you, and if junior petites are too short-waisted or pinched on you, go to another department which carries regular junior or standard sizes.

## Appropriate Clothes

After you've decided what looks well on you, your next question is "Will it look well where I'm going?" I imagine that innumerable times, when you were dressing to go out, your mother has said, "I think your green cotton would be just right." And you've replied, "But, Mom, everyone's wearing levis." Well, I'm on your side. Nothing is worse than going to a party overdressed, or in something that makes you stick out like a sore thumb. Remember, however, Mother is occasionally right, so be on the safe side and call your hostess to find out just what the uniform of the day is.

PARTIES

When a written invitation says "Casual," shorts, slacks, or skirts are in order. Choose whichever is most becoming and most comfortable. Stand out from the crowd with your color combination, your big bright piece of jewelry pinned to your sweater, or your new-length skirt.

"Informal" generally means a dress rather than shorts or slacks. A skirt and blouse or sweater may be acceptable, but if it's a big party it probably means a dressy wool in winter or a cotton or silk in summer. Flats, sandals, or loafers go with the pants outfit or with skirts, but wear heels with the dresses.

DANCES

Some proms, most debuts, and special balls require a formal evening dress, which means a floor-length dress with a low-cut neckline, and narrow shoulder straps or none at all. Elbow-length (or higher) gloves are worn, and they do look and feel terribly elegant. The invitations will say "Formal dress" or possibly, though rarely, "White tie."

Invitations to club dances, dances in private homes, and school dances may say "Formal" or "Black tie." At most of these parties, you would be overdressed in your real "ball gown" but you must wear an evening dress. It may be high- or low-necked, floor-length or short, depending on current styles, with or without sleeves.

At informal dances you wear anything from a short cotton shift to a floor-length skirt and a blouse. You generally know by instinct or experience what sort of party it will be—if you don't, discuss it with some of your friends who will be going too.

CLOTHES FOR DATES

There can't be any hard and fast rules about clothes for dates because it depends on what kind of a date it is. But you'll feel a lot more comfortable if you think to ask, when you get the invitation, what you'll be doing. Who wants to turn up at the bowling alley in high heels and a tight skirt? If you're double dating, check with the other girl. She'll be as pleased as you to know that you'll be in tune.

Here are a few suggestions which apply in a variety of situations.

Unless you're going to participate in a sport which requires a special outfit, wear skirts. Even for a movie date, a boy likes his girl to look feminine.

Wear jewelry conservatively. Wooden and enamel pins or earrings are right with casual clothes; gold jewelry or a strand of pearls is better with a dress.

Sandals and flats are prettier and more feminine than loafers or sneakers, even with slacks or shorts. Shoes with heels are more flattering to the legs, but heels go with dresses—never with pants.

Enormous pocketbooks are a nuisance and tend to bump into and annoy your date. On the other hand, carry one large enough to hold your make-up and other essentials, so that he won't have to load his pockets with your necessities.

If you're going to the city, wear short, spotless white gloves. They give an air of chic to the simplest costume.

### DINING OUT

When you're going out to dinner with your parents, you should consider the fact that your appearance will reflect on your whole family. Even if the waiter isn't going to turn you away, you must change out of your school clothes into something fresh, and certainly you shouldn't wear slacks or shorts. There are exceptions—drive-ins, for instance—but I'm talking about real, honest-to-goodness restaurants.

It's a real compliment when a boy asks you out to dinner, so repay him by making him proud of you. Choose your prettiest "afternoon dress," jewelry to go with it, and pumps rather than flats. This is an occasion to use a little eye make-up and a touch of perfume—in other words, show him you appreciate his invitation.

### SCHOOL

Skirts and blouses or sweaters are the most comfortable and appropriate clothes for school. They're practical too, because by varying the combinations you have a number of different outfits. Dress up the blouse with a gold or enamel pin on the collar, or wear a string of wooden beads with the sweater. Choose skirts that are easy-fitting and not too short, so that they won't ride up badly when you sit down. Simple dresses are fine, and they provide a change when you're sick of the same old routine. Flats, including loafers and saddle shoes when they're in style, are the best shoes. Carry a purse for your cosmetics and accessories: either a small one which can lie on top of your pile of books, or one with a shoulder strap.

If you're faced with looking for a job in the near future, you'll feel more at ease if you know you look *right*. Prospective employers aren't interested in seeing how chic or stylish you can be; they're more interested in the neatness and appropriateness of your costume and your grooming. Wear a dress or a neat suit—not a skirt and sweater—and shoes with medium heels. Neither loafers nor spike heels are appropriate for job hunting. Don't load on the make-up—the interviewer wants to see the "real" you. He's not impressed by someone obviously looking for a beau, but by a girl who looks as if she intended to stay for a while.

You will find more tips on clothes for job hunters, your traveling wardrobe, and party clothes in the chapters on those subjects.

# 8 How About the Men?

Etiquette books always seem to be directed at the females, and I find that somewhat strange because males are interested in the subject. Witness the evidence—the many well-mannered, well-groomed boys and men in the world! It is a fact that the distaff side is largely responsible for our social life, such as giving parties and running households, but some parts of etiquette belong strictly to the men. And this section is about one of these parts—an attractive masculine appearance.

## *The Personal Hygiene Habit*

Boys from thirteen to nineteen need to spend a great deal of time on personal hygiene. Some of you mature before you're thirteen, and because you look older than you are people expect more of you.

Whether you enjoy or hate it, cultivate the shaving *habit!* Nothing looks worse than a "five o'clock shadow" which starts at seven— A.M. It's hard to believe when your beard first starts growing that it's not going to stop. But it isn't, and while you may only have to shave once or twice a week at first, it won't be long before you should be doing it daily, or at the very least every other day. The important thing is to make it a habit, like brushing your teeth. If you don't have to shave *every* day, set a definite schedule of when you should do so, and then stick to it.

Along with a grubby beard go tattletale-gray hands and faces. Dirt anywhere is unattractive, but on your face and hands it shows. It's vital for your complexion, too, that you wash your face with soap at least twice a day to get rid of the oily deposit that causes bad cases of pimples. Teen-age boys also tend to have very active sweat glands, so if you don't want to find out the embarrassing way what even your best friend won't tell you, a daily shower is a *must.*

## *Hair Care*

Without going into the merits of long hair or short hair, let me stress the importance of clean hair. No matter what style you choose, "greasy kid stuff" won't improve it. Keep your hair clean; washing at least once a week is essential, and if you use a preparation to keep down cowlicks or to hold hair out of your eyes, choose one which is not greasy, and which doesn't look as if you were wearing patent leather on your head.

## Fashion Plate or Fink?

When boys are with other boys or girls of their own age, I don't think it's too important *what* they wear. If the other kids in town wear white Levis and sneakers, fine, wear them too. If black cords and cowboy boots are the thing, O.K. Open-necked shirts, turtlenecks, T-shirts, or imported Italian knits are all great if—and this is important—they fit properly and are clean!

There isn't any charm in looking greasy and grubby, and I doubt if your girl thinks that spots on your shirt, jacket, or pants really do much for your appeal. So when you're with your gang wear whatever they're wearing and be comfortable—just let it do the best it can for you!

When you're taking a girl on a date, it's another story. No matter what she may say to the contrary, there isn't a girl in the world who isn't flattered when her date dresses up a little for her. If it's a first date and you want to make some points, a clean shirt will score a lot higher than the T-shirt you played ball in all afternoon.

Naturally, if you're going to bowl or ice skate, or watch some sporting events, you'll wear whatever clothes fit the occasion. But if you're taking your date to a restaurant for dinner, or to the theater (should she be so lucky!) or even to a movie, the occasion will seem a lot more special if you dress up for it.

Going out with your parents is another occasion for looking especially nice. It will be worth the effort to see your mother's face light up when you appear, clean, combed, and wearing a jacket and tie.

When you receive a written or engraved invitation to a party or dance, check to see if it tells you what you're expected to wear. If it says "Black tie," that means you wear a tuxedo, and if you don't have one you beg, borrow, or rent one. Unless you have succeeded in getting one by the appointed date, call to say that you must break the date. "Semi-formal" sometimes means a suit, but you can usually get away with a madras jacket or a blazer. "Informal" is just that—sweater, slacks, jeans, or shorts—but remember, it *is* a party, so work a little harder at your color combination and your choice of shirt, etc. "Informal" can also mean ties and sports jackets, so if you're in doubt check with the host or hostess, or a friend who is likely to know.

Your parents have undoubtedly been telling you for years how important your appearance is, but the first time you may agree with them is the day you start job hunting. You'll find they were right. Sure, you can slouch in the office door with your hands in your pockets, your shirt tail out, and chewing gum, and if help is needed badly enough you'll possibly land a job. But even if you do, your employer won't be favorably impressed. The boys who made an effort to look well groomed when they applied for positions will be the ones who are considered for raises and more responsible jobs.

Your clothes don't have to be expensive, but your trousers should have a crease, your shoes should be shined, your shirt collar must be spotless, and do wear a conservative tie. Your hair, hands, nails, and face must be immaculately clean. If you can bring yourself to take a trip to the barber beforehand, remember that almost every adult in the business world likes to *see* a boy's eyes and ears, and some offices won't even consider an applicant who comes in with hair down to his shoulders.

No matter what job you're after, the general impression you make is important. And that impression is only favorable if you are clean, neatly groomed, and obviously making a real effort to look your best.

# THE ART OF
# CONVERSATION

# 9 Introductions

## Casual Introductions

It would be a total waste of time—both yours and mine—for me to give you a complicated formula for introducing one of your own friends to another. In a nutshell, you can, and probably will, just say the two names. You may, if you wish, put a "this is" or "I'd like you to know" in between. "Mary Witherspoon, John Fogarty," or "Mary, this is [or, "I'd like you to meet"] John Fogarty. John, this is Mary Witherspoon." Using the latter form, you do, of course, have to repeat "Mary" (or "John") in order to give the last name, so it's simpler just to say the two names. The only rule you should try to remember and follow is that in a mixed introduction of people of the same age group, the girl's name always comes first.

What will probably happen is that John will say something like "Joe, this is the blond I told you about," and Joe may not learn her name for days. But she'll be flattered, and Joe won't mind, so it doesn't really matter much among friends.

## A Little More Formality

However, there are times—in school, at formal parties, or on other occasions—when the forms are more important, and you should know them. Even within your own age group, you stick to the rule about the girl's name coming first, you use both first and last names, and you add, if possible, a phrase of identification. "Debbie, this is Ann Weinberg. She just moved here from Chicago. Ann, I'd like you to meet Debbie Parder, our class president," gives both girls a hint of something they can use to start an easy conversation.

The response to these elementary introductions is equally simple. "Hello" or even "Hi," followed by the name of the other person, is adequate. Repeating the name is a good gimmick for fixing it in your own mind, and it acknowledges to the others that you've caught it. It's also more polite than a plain "Hi." You can always add a little phrase such as "I'm awfully glad to meet you. Joan has told me so much about you." Don't, however, chop it up into "Please t'meecha"—and don't say it at all unless it's true. When you really mean it, your enthusiastic tone and manner are what give the statement the ring of truth.

## When Adults Are Involved

Now we come to a different situation—introductions involving older people. The rules are simple enough but, unfotunately, they are fraught with contradictions.

*Basic rule #1:* A man is always introduced TO a woman.

This is done by actually using the word *to*—"Mr. Jacoby, I'd like to introduce you TO Mrs. Howard"—or, in the simplest forms of introduction, putting the woman's name first.

"Mrs. Wallauer, Mr. Coleridge."
"Mrs. McClellan, I'd like you to meet Dr. Foster."

*Basic rule #2:* A younger person is always introduced TO an older person.

"Dr. Foster, this is my brother Bob."
"Professor Brown, do you know my roommate, Bob Henderson?"
"Mrs. Sudbay, I'd like you to meet Sue Youngblood."

*Basic rule #3:* A less important person—man or woman—is introduced TO a more important one. Church officials, members of nobility, heads of state, or those in very high positions are obviously "important." But on the whole this is a sticky rule, because you may have a rough time deciding who *is* more important.

"Bishop Farthing, may I introduce our neighbor, Professor Fiske?"
"Governor Lake, this is Miss Bowman."
"Professor Edwards, I'd like you to meet my fiancé, John Gordon."

## Complications

So much for the relatively easy, cut-and-dried introductions. At this point, let's discuss those that are more involved. I believe the best way I can help you where the situation becomes complicated by a mixture of age, importance, and sex is to give you as many examples of acceptable forms as possible. Remember that the explanatory phrase always helps. Also remember that forms such as "I'd like you to meet" or "Do you know?" are useful, because, except for the order of the names, they avoid actually introducing one person *to* another. Family relationships should be included: "My stepfather, Mr. Dubois," "My aunt, Mrs. Hill."

In introducing a member of your family to an outsider, it is more courteous to imply that the other person is the important one, and it also makes for a simpler form if you can put the "My sister Eileen" at the end, even though she is being introduced to a man.

> "Professor Higgins, I'd like you to meet my uncle, Mr. Carew."
> "Dr. Phillips, do you know my cousin, Francine Sawtelle?"

When you are introducing your mother or father to someone who surely knows your name, and therefore your parents', you need not actually say the name: "Mother, this is Miss Dewey, the science teacher I've told you so much about."

A step-relative's name, because it is often different, should be mentioned: "Mrs. Edmonds, this is my stepfather, Mr. Jacobs."

## It's Simple, Really

If you read this section carefully, I'm sure you'll find that making introductions isn't really terribly complicated. You're pretty safe if you mention the a. woman's, b. older person's, c. most important name first. If you do slip and, for example, start out with the man's name, it's easy to make it come out right by simply adding, "I'd like to introduce you TO Mrs. Gordon."

At a general gathering with no family involved, any one of the following forms is correct and natural:

"Mrs. Mooney, I'd like you to meet Dr. Jones, our dentist."
"Mrs. Suitor, do you know my roommate, Mary Stokely?"
"Miss Frick, Lieutenant Jones."
"Mr. Daniels, have you met my house guest, Bob Friend?"

Always give the name which the newly introduced pair will use in speaking to each other. Just because you call your stepfather by his first name is no reason that your roommate should. To him, he's your stepfather, Mr. Jacobs. In introducing two older people, you should not use their first names, even though they may soon be calling each other Bob and Frank. For you to speak of them in that way would definitely not be a respectful form of introduction.

I don't know why this whole subject causes such panic, but it does—in all of us. People have been known to forget their own brothers' or sisters' names when faced with introducing them. If that happens to you there is not much you can do except throw yourself on the mercy of the court and admit you've had a temporary lapse of memory, but if you're the one being introduced, *speak up!* You can save the whole situation by quickly saying your name: "I'm Sue, Joan's sister."

# 10 Colorful Language vs. Poor Taste

## The Tone of Your Voice

Before going into the subject of words, I want to mention the importance of the voice that says them. No matter how interesting or colorful your language may be, it doesn't come through well if your voice is too loud, too harsh, or too high.

1. A low voice is definitely more appealing than a high-pitched squeak.
2. A soft voice is more attractive than a raucous one.
3. The person who enunciates clearly and reasonably slowly is easier—and more fun—to listen to than the one who runs all the words together into an indivisible jumble.
4. Variation of tone is important. Nothing is duller than a monotone! Tempo and pitch must change somewhat or your stories will fall flat.

You may well say that these statements are obvious, and probably they are, but then why don't more people work at cultivating a pleasant voice? It is a great shame, because a pleasant speaking voice is distinctive—and it's easy to acquire if you'll bear in mind the four points mentioned above. But walk down any city street in the United States and almost every voice you hear will be blurring, slurring, twanging, or shouting.

Actually most of us don't know how we sound, and it's usually an awful shock the first time we hear our own voices recorded. Anyone who cares at all can easily arrange to make a recording and listen to his own speech on tape. Many of you have recorders and the means to play a tape, but if you don't know anyone who has one, almost every high school has equipment that can be used. Get a group and do it together; I promise you the results can be hilarious—and enlightening!

## Irritating Habits

Haven't you noticed little speech habits or mannerisms accompanying speech that annoy you? Constant knuckle cracking, shuffling, or drumming on the table occur over and over in conversation and are thoroughly irritating. Many of us fall into the habit of repeating a certain phrase ad nauseam. If you can avoid that trap your conversation will improve a lot and actually be more stimulating. The commonest offenses are ones you've all heard:

The hesitating "er" or "eh" at the beginning of a sentence.

The "y'know?" at the end of every phrase.

Simple exclamations like "You said it!" or single words such as "great" or "really" used over and over again.

## Grammatical Booby Traps

There are three or four grammatical usages that one hears constantly which are just plain incorrect. And the correct phrase is neither stilted nor more complicated, so there is every reason to use it. The wrong way and the right way of some common errors follow.

| WRONG | RIGHT |
|---|---|
| He gave a book to John and *I*. | He gave a book to John and *me*. To check yourself, leave out the "John." Would you say, "He gave a book to I?" |
| He *don't* want it. | He *doesn't* want it. Third person singular. |
| If you knock someone down, stop and help *them* up. | "If you knock someone down, stop and help *him* up." Someone is singular. |
| Consensus of opinion. | Consensus. The word means "a collective opinion." I grant that "consensus of opinion" is widely used, but it is redundant, and therefore to be avoided. |

## *Affected Speech*

The very best and most reliable rule for excellent speech is always to choose the most common and simplest English word. A smattering of words from a foreign language can add color, but their use is vastly overdone, and worse, often incorrectly done. An American who has never even been to Italy sounds pretty silly when he regularly replaces "So long" with "*Ciao,*" and the same holds true for "Cheerio" or "*Adiós.*" On the other hand, many foreign words—fiancé, hors-d'oeuvre, padre—have become an accepted part of our speech. The worst mistake is the habit of using a word, English or foreign, when you're not sure of either its pronunciation or meaning.

I know you're apt to speak normally when you're with your own group, but when you meet new people, especially older people, there's an unconscious urge to make a special impression by using flowery language. Believe me, you make a better showing being your natural self.

A list of some of the commonest pitfalls follows, and shows both right and wrong usage:

| AVOID SAYING | USE INSTEAD |
|---|---|
| A lovely *affair*. | A lovely *party*. |
| *Allow* me to help. | *Let* me help. |
| I *arise* at seven. | I *get up* at seven. |
| I will *attend* Mass. | I'll *go to* Mass. |
| Sit on the *davenport*. | Sit on the *couch; sofa*. |
| Full-length *drapes*. | Full-length *curtains; draperies*. |
| He will *endeavor* to. | He will *try* to. |
| He entered the *foyer*. | He entered the *hall*. |
| An *elegant* room. | A *beautiful* room. |
| It's a pretty *gown*. | It's a pretty *evening dress*. |
| Our *home* has five rooms. | Our *house* has five rooms. |
| I bought some *hose*. | I bought some *stockings*. |
| It was a *lovely* dinner. | It was a *delicious* dinner. |
| *Pardon* me. | *Excuse me; I'm sorry; I beg your pardon*. |
| I tried to *purchase*. | I tried to *buy*. |
| That's *sufficient*. | That's *enough*. |
| She *visited* with her friend. | She *chatted; talked with* her friend. |

In addition, there are some words we use for the opposite effect—to make ourselves more "folksy." This is reverse snobbery and, if it isn't a person's natural manner of speech, it is in just as poor taste as trying to appear loftily elegant.

| WRONG WORD | RIGHT WORD |
|---|---|
| She met his *folks*. | She met his *family*. |
| I *reckon* so. | I *think* so. |

## *Regional Variations*

Personally, I love to talk with people from the Deep South or the Far West, for the differences from my pronunciation and word usage are fascinating. Nothing more clearly shows a narrow-minded and provincial attitude than a snicker at the speech of someone who comes from another part of the United States. Tolerant amusement or entertaining comparison is another matter; together you can get a good laugh out of some of the misunderstandings and confusions that occur.

The Brooklynite who pronounces "boil" as "berl," the Chicagoan who eats "chawklut" candy, and the Southerner who says "Ah'm goin' to Tayxas" are all pronouncing words as they are said in their areas. They are, therefore, perfectly correct and should not be subject to ridicule. Words even have different meanings in different sections. In one town, the clerk puts your groceries in a "bag," in another town it's a "sack." Tennis shoes are "sneakers" in the East, "tenny-runners" in some parts of the West. And in some areas girls don't say they're going to "set" their hair, they're going to "roll" it. It all adds up to variety and color, so don't knock it—enjoy it!

## *Slang*

If you think I'm going to say you shouldn't use slang, you've got me all wrong. In fact, if it weren't for my editors, this book would have more of it! According to the dictionary, slang is "Language, words, or phrases of a vigorous, colorful, facetious, or taboo nature, invented for specific occasions or uses, or derived from the unconventional use of the standard vocabulary." With the exception of "taboo," how could anyone object to any of that?

The fact that slang is apt, forceful, and colorful not only makes it irresistible but is the reason it adds so much to language. However, a warning: to be an asset, slang must be up-to-date and absolutely applicable, and it must not be overdone. The danger is in becoming dependent on it and neglecting your more formal conversation. Use slang while it's current, but don't slip into a rut and use the same expression or word over and over again. Then it becomes irritating to others and difficult to drop.

## Jokes and Jokes

One of the most flagrant violations of etiquette that I know is the telling of insulting ethnic jokes. The whole purpose of this book is to convince you that good manners are based on principles of kindness and thoughtfulness. Ethnic jokes, when they are based on derogatory commentary about other races or nationalities, violate those principles completely. If you can draw a laugh only by insulting other people, better leave the storytelling to someone else. Although a member of the particular nationality may not actually be present, you never know if your listeners have friends or relatives belonging to that group, and they may be more hurt than if they were the target themselves.

As for "dirty" jokes, I know you'll probably tell or at least listen to them, so I'd like to make one plea. When you're the narrator, avoid the use of really offensive words. Many people don't object to an off-color story, but everyone with the slightest sense of good taste dislikes the use of four-letter words. They are rarely essential to the story, and are used entirely in an attempt to shock. The line between what is funny and what is in good or bad taste is often hard to draw, so when you're in doubt, the safest course is to stay clear of "dirty" jokes.

## Increase Your Vocabulary

A good vocabulary is a sign of education, and it also makes you much more interesting to talk to. It's so boring to hear the same word used over and over again—a nice house, a nice date, the meal was nice, and on and on. There are innumerable alternatives— "lovely," "attractive," "delicious," or just plain "fun" or "good"— which will save your comments from monotony.

Reading is the best way to increase your vocabulary. Read anything you can lay your hands on! Keep a list of new words. Look them up in the dictionary when you come across them, and write down the definitions. The mere act will help to fix them in your memory. Listen to teachers, your parents, good television programs and movies, and when you hear a new word you like try using it right away, before it's gone from your mind. But don't go overboard. Make sure you understand and can pronounce a word before you adopt it. Plain speech which sounds unaffected is far more attractive than self-conscious use of a recently broadened vocabulary.

# CORRESPONDENCE

# 11 Personal Letters

When you are living at home, surrounded by family and friends, it doesn't matter much, except as a matter of status, how much mail you receive. But, as soon as you are at school, college, in the army, at camp, or even on a vacation trip, mail becomes terribly important. As a link with your family and friends, and to tell you what's going on at home, there's nothing that can take the place of a good letter.

## Make Your Letters Talk

The letters that are the most fun are those written as if the writer were right there talking to you. There are a number of little tricks that will give your letters this effect, and once you get used to writing the way you talk, you'll find letter writing much easier.

Punctuation adds interest—just as a change in the tone of your voice does. Underline words, capitalize them, use exclamation points and dashes. Consider the difference between these two sentences:

"We went to a dance last night and it was a great party."

"We went to a dance last night—*what* a party!"

Use the phrases you normally do in talking, not stilted or formal ones.

Insert, occasionally, the name of the person you're writing to. It gives the feeling that your news is of special interest to the one who receives your letter.

The use of contractions is perfectly correct. You sound like a grammar text if you write, "I will not" for "I won't," or "I am so glad" for "I'm so glad."

If you type easily and well, and especially if your writing is illegible, by all means use a typewriter. But, at the same time, remember that your handwriting lends a personal touch that a machine can't give. Whether the letter is typewritten or not, *always* sign your name by hand.

Don't forget to answer questions asked of you in a letter you received previously.

Add little drawings or illustrations wherever you can, and enclose clippings and jokes—they do a lot to pep up a run-of-the-mill letter.

And last—don't dwell over what you're writing. Decide what you want to say and write it quickly. It will come out much more naturally, as if you were really talking.


## Dates and Addresses

The date, on writing paper that bears your address, is placed at the upper right side of the page. On personal letters, all that you need write is "Tuesday," or "September 1."

It is not necessary to write out your address if you are using a plain sheet of paper. Unless you have a special reason, it is only required on the envelope. If you do wish to include it inside, it goes in the lower left corner, and the date may go there too, just above the address.


## The Envelope

Use either of these forms:

Miss Harriet Browder          Miss Harriet Browder
10 East Linden Street          10 East Linden Street
Port Chester, New York 10580   Port Chester, New York 10580

On formal correspondence you do not abbreviate "Street" or the name of the state.

The Post Office requests that a return address be written in the upper left corner on the front of an envelope. It should include your complete address and zip code.

## *Better Left Unsaid*

Unless it's absolutely necesssary, don't write about bad news. If you must, be sure that you include all the information you can, because unanswered questions about the situation will only cause additional anxiety.

Don't ever write a letter that would embarrass you should it fall into the wrong hands. Remember that once the word is written it's there for anyone to see, and can come back to haunt you after many moons have passed. Those of you who have read the *Rubáiyát of Omar Khayyám* may remember the famous stanza:

The Moving Finger writes; and, having writ,
Moves on: nor all your Piety nor Wit
  Shall lure it back to cancel half a Line,
Nor all your Tears wash out a Word of it.

If you write to your boy or girl friend in a more or less emotional vein, keep your letter overnight and read it once more in the morning. If it still sounds right and says just what you meant it to, mail it. More often than you can imagine, however, what you wrote in a moment of anger, boredom, or loneliness, or just in an extra-affectionate mood, can sound pretty silly in the cold light of day.

Remember that the tone of your voice, which can save a cutting remark from giving offense, is not present in the written word. So beware of remarks which are amusing when spoken, but which can be insulting or derogatory when written.

## *Starts and Finishes*

The following applies only to letters to friends you don't know very well, and to older people. To your family and close friends, it couldn't matter less how you start or finish; anything goes.

When writing less intimate letters, the good old standbys, "Dear Bill" and "Love, Jane," are still the standard phrases. To older family members, you can vary your endings: "With much love" or "Affectionately." The latter is perfect, by the way, for friends of your parents.

Girls never use "Miss" in their signatures on a personal letter. You sign "Sally" or "Sally Lord," depending on whether the receiver will know who "Sally" is. Boys follow the same rule: "Jim" or "Jim Banks."

## Your Equipment

If you possibly can, keep two kinds of writing paper—one box of full-size sheets, either single or double, and one box of fold-over, note-size paper. The first is fine for your chatty letters and for business letters. The second is ideal for thank-you notes, condolence notes, invitations, acceptances, and regrets.

The style of your stationery is up to you—papers come in such pretty colors, with or without borders, that your choice is almost unlimited. A monogram is handsome, but your name and address printed at the top is more helpful. Occasionally a monogram is engraved in the upper left-hand corner, and an address in the right. A simple, legible monogram is best—some are so curlicued and swirled that it is impossible to make out the letters. Unmarried girls do not use "Miss" before their names on printed paper, although it is used on a printed address on the envelope, and on visiting cards. Neither boys nor men ever use "Mr." on their stationery.

Ask your mother or your grandmother to give you your own calling cards, for a birthday or Christmas—they're more practical than you may realize. Not because they are still used for calling (unless you are a member of the diplomatic corps or in the service) but because they are the nicest cards to send with gifts, especially wedding gifts. When enclosing one with a birthday or Christmas present to someone you know well, you cross out the "Miss." Whether you cross it out or not, you may add a word or two, such as, "Best of luck" or "With lots of love." When you give a birthday present to a member of your own group, you will undoubtedly buy a humorous card to go with it. But for presents to older people, and on a formal occasion such as a wedding, humor is not generally appropriate and calling cards are perfect. The store where you order them will tell you the correct size (approximately 2¼ by 3 inches) and show you samples of type. Choose a simple type—Shaded Roman or Script—and your formal name, not a nickname, is correct.

Informals are fold-over cards, slightly larger than visiting cards, engraved with your name. Young people don't have much need for them, as they are used mostly for somewhat formal invitations and answers to them. They can, however, replace notepaper for thank-you and sympathy notes, as they are just large enough to go through the mail.

## Christmas Cards

If your Christmas-card list is long, and you're feeling rich, you may want to have your name printed on your cards. Do *not* use "Miss." If you are universally known by a nickname, use it, along with your last name.

When your nickname is something like "Snookie" rather than a contraction or shortening, stick to your correct name, but a signature such as "Cindy Fuller" is friendlier than "Cynthia Fuller." Actually, I recommend unprinted cards; the handwritten "Cindy," or "Cindy Fuller," depending on how well you know the recipient, is much more personal.

# 12 Letters That Must Be Written

It would be a great mistake to try to give you a set formula for letters of thanks or of condolence. In the first place, circumstances and relationships vary too much, and, in the second place, they express personal feelings that should come from your heart.

Certainly in the case of close friends, you know exactly what you want to say. However, from time to time, it is necessary to write to a barely known relative or to an older family friend, and it is sometimes hard to know how to begin. In a questionnaire sent to hundreds of young people, we asked what sort of help they would like when faced with these difficult letters, and the following examples are a result of the requests.

## Thank-You Notes

*Don't use printed cards.* No matter how "elegant" you think they look, they are the lazy man's way out, and show no real appreciation at all. Your note may be just two or three lines long, but it must be personal and it must sound as if you really mean it.

*Christmas present* (and be sure to write *before* the end of your Christmas vacation):

Dear Aunt Jo,
    The jewel box you sent me is absolutely terrific! I found earrings and a bracelet in my stocking, and now, thank heavens, I'll have a place to keep them and my other jewelry where they won't be all jumbled around and scratched, as they were in my old cardboard box.
    Our Christmas was very hectic, as usual, but great fun, and I hope yours was, too.
    Thank you again and again, and until we see you,
Loads of love,<br>Fran

*Birthday present* (to be written within a week):

Dear Mrs. Gordon,

Mother, or someone, must have told you that my favorite color is blue! The sweater you gave me is just gorgeous, and what's more it goes with almost everything I own.

Thank you so much for thinking of me, and I'll drop in and say "Hello" when I get home for vacation.

Affectionately,
Sue

*Graduation present* (write before, or within a week after, the ceremony):

Dear Jane:

You honestly do have a genius for choosing the most perfect presents! I just can't thank you enough for the evening bag. You knew, of course, my graduation dress would be white, but how did you know I'd been desperately hunting for a purse to take to the dance that night?

I'm so pleased that you and Joe will be able to come—can't wait to see you both. Thanks again, and

Much love,
Helen

*A note in addition to verbal thanks* (written a day or two later):

Dear Uncle Ted,

Even though I gave you a hug and a kiss to thank you for the book you gave me on Christmas day, I wanted to write and tell you how much I am enjoying reading it.

Thanks again—your presents are *always* the greatest!

Much love,
Sally

*For a gift of money* (write within a week):

Dear Uncle Tom,

This year, especially, your check was the ideal present! I'm saving up for a tape recorder, and without an occasional gift like yours I'd be old and gray before I could ever make it.

Thanks ever so much—it really brought my recorder closer by months!

Love,<br>Bob

## Bread-and-Butter Letters

After a visit at the home of one of your very best friends, a bread-and-butter letter need only be written to her mother. But if your friend is only semi-close, it's a good idea to write her too.

The letters need be no longer than thank-you letters but they must be written *immediately*—within three days after the end of the visit. Try to mention at least one special event, and even if you were bored to death the whole time, don't let it show through!

Dear Barbs,

I certainly hated to leave Cape Cod and come back to the hot, old city after such a terrific weekend. Everything was great, starting with the picnic Friday night and ending with the round-robin tennis tournament Sunday, but I think the high spot was the Country Fair on Saturday. That was an experience I'll *never* forget!

Thank you so much for asking me, and call me as soon as you get back to town—I'll be anxious to hear what's gone on the rest of the summer.

Loads of love,<br>Jane

Much more important than your note to Barbs is your thank-you to Barb's mother:

Dear Mrs. Lamb,

How can I thank you? You and Mr. Lamb were so good to have me—and the rest of the gang—up for such a long weekend. You gave us a marvelous time and I just hope we weren't too much for you and your lovely house.

Everything was perfect, but the best of all was the Country Fair—I wish you had come along to see us city slickers trying all the games, rides, and goodies.

Mother sends her regards, and I certainly do thank you both again for a wonderful weekend.

Affectionately,<br>Flora

Some visits are simply the result of your hostess's having offered to help a friend by putting up one or more young people for the night of a party or dance. Even these visits, for which you may have received no invitation, but have simply been told, "You'll be staying at Mrs. Goldfarb's house," require a bread-and-butter letter.

Dear Mrs. Goldfarb,

Thank you ever so much for letting me stay at your house the night of Joanie's dance. It was great meeting you and your family, and you certainly went all out to make me feel at home.

I hope I'll have a chance to come back to Charleston, but until I do, thanks again.

Very sincerely,
Harry Johnson

It is not necessary to write to thank your hostess for a dinner, or other party, but if you've had an extra-good time, and want to, it is always appreciated.

Dear Mrs. Farthingham,

Your dinner party for Sue was such fun—I just wanted to write you and tell you how much I enjoyed it. Everyone is talking about what a great party it was. Thank you so much for asking me.

Affectionately,
Linda

## Letters of Condolence

It is very difficult to write a sincere letter to someone you hardly know about the death of someone you may not have known at all. But there are times when it is necessary, and the following notes may suggest something that is both brief and sincere.

Dear Cousin Mary,

I was really shocked to hear of Joe's sudden death. Although we saw each other rarely, we always had such a good time together when we did, and I liked him so much, that I realize what a terrible loss this is for you.

Please believe you have my very deepest sympathy.

With much love,
Madeline

Dear Bob,

I know that a few written words can't mean much at a time like this, but I wanted to let you know that I have been thinking of you, and that you have my deepest sympathy.

If there is *anything* at all I can do for you, please send me the word.

Jack

Dear Mrs. Farber,

I just wanted to tell you how terribly sorry I was to receive Mother's letter telling me of Mr. Farber's death. You both have always been so good to me that I feel as if I have lost a member of my own family.

Please accept my sympathy and love.

Julie Burns

Printed sympathy cards do not require an answer, but handwritten letters of condolence must be acknowledged. The note may be very short, it may be written by another member of the family if there are too many for one person to cope with, and it may be sent some time after the funeral. Sons and daughters often help a widowed parent by taking over some of this duty.

In reply to letters written to you, you might say:

Dear Joanne,

Your letter arrived at a time when I really needed the support of my friends. It is a great comfort to know how many people loved Dad, and I want to thank you for writing.

Much love,
Betty

When you're writing the letter for your mother or father, the wording is a little different.

Dear Mrs. Howard,

Mother has asked me to write and tell you how grateful she was for your sweet letter. I would like to add my thanks to you for writing—notes like yours have been such a great help to all of us at this time.

Sincerely,
Marie Faulkner

## *Letters of Apology*

Every once in a while something unfortunate occurs which makes it necessary to write a letter of apology. Sometimes it is easier to do this than to telephone or to make the apology face to face.

Dear Mrs. Franklin,

I do want to apologize for having let you know so late last week that I couldn't come for dinner on Saturday. I simply had the date of my return to college mixed up, and thought I didn't have to be back until Sunday. Please forgive me. I do hope it didn't upset the plans for your dinner too much.

Sincerely,
Ruth Jones

Dear Mrs. Harper,

I want to apologize for the carelessness of one of my guests who parked on your lawn during my party last weekend. I have no idea whose car was involved, but please have the damage repaired and send the bill to me.

I will see that my friends are more careful in the future, and I am very sorry it happened.

Sincerely,
Lucille Melton

# 13 Business Letters

The older you get, the more business letters you'll have to write—
to schools or colleges, to apply for a job, to order from a catalogue,
to make a hotel reservation, and so on.

## Letter Form

Typewritten business letters are preferred because of their legi-
bility, but there is no rule that says they must be typed. Handwritten letters follow the same forms, but they must be neat and
clear.

The date is at the upper right and is written "September 12,
1967."

The name and address of the person to whom you are writing
(including his title if he has one) go at the left of the page, and
two lines are left between his address and the salutation.

When the letter is typed, new paragraphs are not necessarily in-
dented, but a double space is always left between paragraphs.

Your name is typed below your handwritten signature.

## Openings and Closings

If your know the name of the man to whom you are writing, you
address him "Dear Mr. Hollowell." If you are writing to an organization and do not have a specific name to address your letter to,
you start out "Dear Sirs" or "Dear Sir" (or "Gentlemen")—whichever fits the case. In these circumstances a woman is addressed as
"Dear Madam."

In writing to a woman's organization, a club, or girls' school, perhaps you may not know whom to address and the plural form

"Dear Mesdames," which corresponds to "Dear Sirs," is very bad form. Therefore, address your envelope to the organization and put "Att.: Secretary" or "Att.: The President" in the lower left-hand corner. You may then correctly use the singular—"Dear Madam."

"Very truly yours," "Yours truly," "Sincerely," or "Sincerely yours" are all correct endings. Both boys and girls use first and last names in the handwritten signature. If the letter is typed, the girl types "Miss Elizabeth Jones" below the handwritten name; if the whole letter is written by hand, she may put "(Miss)" before her signature. A boy never uses a title.

When a girl is writing in an official capacity, for a club, for instance, she may add a line below her typewritten name: "Secretary, Jones High School Girls' Club."

## Sample Letters

JAMES BENTLEY
101 Wacker Avenue
Tenafly, New Jersey 10486

March 7, 1967

Mr. Herbert Farmer
Director of Admissions
Heilbrunn College
Pool City, Utah 25901

Dear Mr. Farmer:

I am planning to take summer courses in agriculture and have been told that your college offers exactly those subjects in which I am interested.

I would like very much to visit Heilbrunn the weekend of April tenth, and wonder if it would be possible to arrange an interview with you at that time.

I hope to hear from you soon.

Sincerely yours,
James Bentley

When ordering from a store by mail, use their order form if possible. If not, be sure to include name and descriptions of article, quantity, price, how paid for, how you want things sent, your address, and the date.

June 6, 1967

Bloomingdale's
Stamford
Connecticut 20876

Dear Sirs:

Please send me by parcel post the following articles from your catalogue:

#4430—1 pr. leather gloves, brown, size 6½ $6.00
#4576—2 boxes nylon stockings, beige tone, size 9½ $6.00
#4781—1 cotton bathrobe, pink, size 10 $8.95

I am enclosing a money order for $21.95, which includes shipping
charges as noted in the catalogue.

My address is:

Miss Jean Simons
Rarepenny Road
Richmond, Virginia 62987

Very truly yours,
Miss Jean Simons

If you wish to make a good impression on a prospective employer, your letter must be neatly typed or written, and must include all pertinent information.

June 3, 1967

Mr. John Briarcliff, Personnel Manager
Hart and Benchley
201 State Street
Boston, Massachusetts 60739

Dear Mr. Briarcliff:

In answer to your advertisement in the classified section of the
Boston Globe, I would like to apply for the position of stenographer
in your firm.

I am seventeen years old, and secretary of our junior class at Cam-
bridge High School. I have taken two years of shorthand and typing
and can type at the rate of fifty words per minute. I worked as a
stenographer in my uncle's office last summer, filling in for his regular
girls when they were on vacation. My uncle is Mr. John Schaffer,
President of the Bingham Lock Company, 75 Main Avenue, Linden,
Massachusetts.

If you feel that I would be qualified to fill the position which is open, please write to me at

> 703 Davis Lane
> Hingham
> Massachusetts 60740

and I will be delighted to make an appointment with you at your convenience.

> Sincerely yours,
> Miss Eleanor Hobbs

# 14 Invitations, Acceptances, and Regrets

## *Invitations*

At this point in your life you will probably not have to send out formal invitations yourself. They are almost invariably sent by parents or an organization, although the party may be in your honor. But, should you plan to give a formal dinner or dance other than a debut party, you may buy already engraved cards which follow the formal wording but leave spaces for the name, date, etc., to be filled in.

> *Miss Mary Howard*
> *requests the pleasure of the company of*
> *Miss June Landers*
> *at a dinner dance*
> *on Saturday, the seventeenth of June,*
> *at 7 o'clock*

*R.s.v.p.*

> *785 Meadow Road*
> *Bloomfield*

If you wish to write formal invitations on plain white cards, you may. They should follow exactly the form of an engraved card.

Miss Mary Howard
requests the pleasure of your company
at dinner before the Assembly
on Saturday, the seventeenth of May,
at seven o'clock

R.s.v.p.

785 Meadow Road
Bloomfield

For all other occasions, you may buy whatever attractive party invitation card is most appropriate. Be sure to put "R.s.v.p." in a bottom corner, and follow it with your telephone number, or your address if no one is likely to be home to take calls. Invitations to informal parties may be telephoned, if you prefer, and that's the surest way of getting a prompt answer. But it does mean the guest won't have a card in hand to remind him of the date, hour, etc.

If you should become involved in giving a shower or a party to which adults are invited, a short handwritten note is a perfect invitation.

July 7

Dear Mrs. Briggs,

I am having a bon voyage luncheon for Sarah on Saturday, the 19th, and would like you to come. It will be at 12:30 at the Shorerock Club, 25 Lindstrom Drive. I hope to see you then.

Sincerely,
Linda Fredericks

R.s.v.p.
16 Mott Street
Bloomfield

## Acceptances and Regrets

Acceptances and regrets to formal invitations are easy to write because they have a set form which, once learned, serves for every one.

*Miss Lucinda Porter*
*accepts with pleasure*
*Mr. and Mrs. Weatherby's*
*kind invitation for*
*Saturday, the nineteenth of April*

*Miss Lucinda Porter*
*regrets that she will be unable to accept*
*Mr. and Mrs. Weatherby's*
*kind invitation for*
*Saturday, the nineteenth of April*

The date should be written out, just as it is on the invitation, but it is not necessary to use Mr. Weatherby's first name.

When you receive a letter from your friend Peggy's mother inviting you, let's say, for a weekend, you should answer it by note rather than telephone—unless, of course, she says, "Please call me."

June 7

Dear Mrs. Porter,
    Thanks so much for your invitation—of course I wouldn't miss the weekend for anything. I'll arrive on the five o'clock train with Gus, and we can take a cab to your house.
    Looking forward to seeing all the Porters on the fifteenth!
Affectionately,<br>Liz

A refusal should include a valid reason, but your note need not be a long one. Rather than just saying, "I have a previous engagement," it is much friendlier to mention what the engagement is— unless there is an excellent reason not to.

"I'm crushed that I can't accept your invitation to dinner, but our whole family is going to the farm that week," or "I can't tell you how disappointed I was to see that your dinner party is on the same night that I have been invited to the theater. Thank you so much for asking me. I know I'll miss a wonderful party."

# EVERYDAY

# MANNERS

# 15 The Telephone—Potential Family Battleground

The telephone is a marvelous instrument, but it has probably caused as many arguments between teen-agers and their parents as any other single object—arguments that could be so easily avoided if you would sit down, talk it over, and agree to a few simple regulations. Remember that Dad pays for the phone, and that gives him and your mother priority.

The most obvious problem, of course, is arriving at what everyone considers a reasonable length of time for a call. In return for your promise to restrict your conversations to an agreed-upon time, your mother should promise not to glare, to strum, or to pick up an extension every minute or two as a hint. The exact duration must be worked out with your parents, but ten minutes should be an absolute maximum. That's certainly long enough to say almost anything in five different ways, and yet it isn't so long that other members of the family will become apoplectic. Even when your parents are out, the length of your call should be limited, because they, or someone else, may be trying to reach your home for a very important reason.

Calling hours should be agreed upon, and stuck to! If your parents object to your leaving the dinner table to take calls (and they have every right to), tell your friends to avoid calling at that hour; if someone does phone, ask him to call back, or offer to call him when dinner's over. If someone else in the family answers the call, it's only fair that they ask, "Who's calling?" and take a message for you. Unless you're such a superior student that you don't have to do homework, certain hours should be set aside for that—during which time you should neither make nor receive calls. In the case of a necessary call to get a school assignment or for some equally legitimate reason, an exception is in order, but *only* to talk about that subject.

A serious telephone *faux pas* is calling very late at night, or very early on weekend mornings. This particular transgression is committed mostly by young people who consider 10 or 11 P.M., when a lot of tired adults are happily sleeping, the shank of the evening. So please tell your friends, unless your parents are night owls, not to call aften ten at night. The shock of waking out of a sound sleep and the fright of that instant thought—"There's been an accident" —are enough to give your parents a heart attack. Weekend morning calls aren't so startling, but it's the one time your parents can sleep late, and you won't be very popular, especially if they've been out the night before, when Susie calls you at eight-thirty to ask what you're going to wear to church.

If your mother and father, out of either desperation or kindness, have installed a separate phone for you (and your brothers and sisters), remember that you're still a member of a family. When your parents are out, answer their phone and take messages for them; in return they should do the same for you.

## *The Smile in Your Voice*

When you talk on the telephone, the impression you create on your listener is, obviously, made entirely through your voice. He can't see your expression or your gestures, so the tone of your voice, quite aside from what you have to say, is all important.

Speak in your natural voice, neither more loudly nor more softly.

Speak clearly. It's much harder to understand a mumble on the phone than when you can see the speaker.

Talk at a normal rate of speed—tumbling your words out does tend to garble them on the phone.

If you want to sound like yourself, don't be a deadpan—use your normal expressions and inflections.

Let your emotions show in your voice: if you're smiling and enthusiastic when you talk, it will come through at the other end.

## *Placing Calls*

There's a right and there's a wrong way to make telephone calls, and the right way is actually easier for everyone—the caller, the operator, and the person called. If you go along with the following suggestions, you'll save time and avoid ruffling anyone's temper.

Be sure you know the correct number, and dial it carefully.

Allow at least six rings before hanging up; your friend may be in the basement, the garden, or the shower, and nothing is more annoying than to race to answer the phone and then find the caller has hung up.

If you don't know a local number, use your telephone book. The information operator has enough to do without being dialed by people who are too lazy to pick up a directory.

When you dial Information, have the necessary information—the initials as well as the last name, and, if possible, the street address of the person whose number you want.

The same holds true for long-distance calls. When you make one on a pay phone, be sure that you have enough change ready. You may ask the operator approximately how much you will need before she places the call. When you make a long-distance call from a friend's house, always ask the operator, in advance, to give you the charges as soon as you finish, and pay your friend then and there. If your girl friend is out of town and you're in the habit of calling her frequently, ask your parents if you may pay them when the charges come in on their bill. A timer is an excellent idea under these circumstances—the amounts add up astronomically when you're oblivious of everything but the one you're talking to!

Back to local calls: When you've dialed your number and heard "Hello" on the other end, put that smile in your voice and say simply, "Hello, is Jane there?" Or, if Jane's mother answers, "Hello, Mrs. Weatherby, this is Julie Sykes. May I speak to Jane?" When Jane answers, you'll undoubtedly just say "Hi" and go on with whatever you called about, but if it's not Jane you're calling, but Fran, whom you don't know *that* well, "Hi, Fran, this is Mary Montgomery" will make it much easier for her. Whenever you call an adult, identify yourself by your full name: "Hello, Mrs. Schwarz, this is Henry Franklin."

If the person you call is not in, it is thoughtful to leave a message—your name and what time you will call again, or a request that he call you. Leave your number, too, if it is not someone who already knows it. I know how furious my daughter gets when she's told that "Some boy called but he didn't leave his name."

## Answering the Phone

A friendly—not annoyed or bored—"Hello" is the best way to answer the phone. If the call is for the one who answers, "Yes, this is Tom" sounds much more natural than "This is he," and friendlier than "Speaking!"

If the call is for someone else in the house, "Just a minute please, I'll call her," is the polite response to "Is Mrs. Jones in?" But don't drop the phone with a bang, or yell, "Mother, telephone!" with the mouthpiece an inch from your lips. If your sister is just putting the last roller in her hair, or your mother has half a minute more to beat the batter before popping the cake in the oven, you needn't go into details, but simply say, "Please hold on, she'll be here in just a minute." Don't leave the caller hanging on the phone, wondering if you've succeeded in getting the message through or whether everyone in the house has died.

When you answer the phone and the call is for someone who is not at home, *write down* any message you're given. That is the *only* way it will surely be delivered correctly. And don't leave it in some obscure spot or by an extension phone that is rarely used. Every family ought to have a bulletin board or scratch pad where each member looks for messages; if you don't have one it's a good idea for a Christmas present for your mother, or put it on your own gift list.

One special note for sitters—either at other homes, or when sitting for your own baby brother or sister. Don't give out information about the family's return time until the caller has satisfactorily identified himself. You may always ask for the name and the message, and then simply say, "May I ask him to call you as soon as he comes in?" This indicates that the adults will be back before long. You can be asking for trouble if you admit you'll be alone in the house until next Monday.

## Party Lines

It is, of course, especially important to limit the length of your calls on a party line. If you have a number of calls to make, space them a few minutes apart so that other users may have a chance to make their calls. Naturally, it's unforgivable to listen in on other conversations, just as it is to listen on another extension in your home. And finally, the only excuse for interrupting anyone on a party line is an extreme—and I *do* mean extreme—emergency.

## Wrong Numbers

When you're on the receiving end, and you've never heard of Theophilus Thistle, simply say, "I'm sorry, you must have the wrong number," or "There's no one here by that name. What number did you want?" It is not necessary to give out your number, so don't do it; that can leave you open to getting "crank" calls.

If you get a wrong number when you make a call, ask, "Is this

Montrose 3-6284?" and you will know whether the mistake was in having the number wrong or in your dialing. If the person called says, "Yes, it is, but Theophilus Thistle doesn't live here," look up the number again. If the response is "No, it isn't," or "You have a wrong number," dial again—but more carefully this time.

## Ending Calls

Among very good friends it certainly doesn't matter who says, "Well, I've got to get back to cleaning up my room . . . etc.," but between mere acquaintances it's the one who makes the call who ends it. Exception: when you're returning a call by request, the other person has the responsibility—the call, after all, was his originally.

## A Few Social Niceties

When you're invited to a party by telephone, don't say, "I'll let you know," unless you can honestly add something like "I'll have to ask Mom if we're staying home or going to the lake on Saturday." Otherwise it sounds as if you want to wait and see if anything better comes along.

Write down the details of a party invitation. It will save you calling back later to ask, "What time did you say your party starts?"

Girls don't call boys. Except:

To return a call by request
To issue or answer an invitation
To give *important* or long-awaited news
To announce a change of plans

Last but not least—don't use the telephone for practical jokes. If your phone rings frequently and the person at the other end hangs up as soon as you answer, it should be reported to the telephone company; they have a special office to handle these situations. It may be a misguided joker, but it could be a burglar looking for an empty house to rob.

# 16 Manners and Driving

## *Courteous Driving*

I honestly believe that recently licensed teen-agers can be among the best drivers in the country. You have just studied your state's traffic laws, you generally have a horror of being arrested and are therefore law-abiding, your reflexes and coordination are excellent, and you really want to drive well. In addition, in most states you are not allowed alcoholic drinks.

So you may not be the main offenders. But—and this is the big problem—a year or two from now, when you've had your license for a while, statistics prove that you will have the highest accident rate of any age group. The old saying "Familiarity breeds contempt" applies to driving. As your confidence grows, you tend to drive faster; you become careless about little habits that add up to safety; and some of you will start to drink. It isn't always the person who is actually drunk who causes the accidents—it can be the one who has had a beer or two or a couple of drinks and is feeling "exhilarated." He can walk a straight line, he isn't seeing double, and his reflexes are all right, but his judgment is affected. He'll take a chance which he ordinarily wouldn't; he'll go faster than he ordinarily would, and so he becomes a real menace on the road.

You have all been swamped with automobile safety rules and suggestions—on the radio, at school, in magazines and pamphlets, and by your parents. I have no intention of repeating what the authorities have told you. Instead, I want to point out to you some acts of plain, old-fashioned courtesy which, when they become an instinctive part of your driving habits, will make people say, "Let's go in Bob's car," or "Let's let Joan drive." As well as making you a more popular chauffeur, they'll make you a safer driver, because as far as automobile manners are concerned safety and courtesy are indivisible—you can't have one without the other.

Would you shove people off a sidewalk, force your way into a line at a box office, or take up more than your own share of the bench in a football stadium? Of course not. And yet in a car some people tend to forget entirely their normal manners and engage in a machine-against-machine competition rather than a person-to-person relationship. Don't let this happen to you. When you are behind the wheel, the car is an extension of yourself, and you should treat other drivers exactly as you would if they—and you— were on foot.

A few of the following suggestions are included in the traffic laws of some states; others are not even mentioned officially. They are really simple things which you often wish other drivers would do for you. Give yourself a little test. Do you (or if you don't have a license yet, would you) invariably extend the following courtesies to fellow drivers?

When you're driving along in a solid line of cars and some poor fellow is trying to turn in from a side road, do you slow down and leave a little space for him to slide in? Or do you cling to the bumper ahead, muttering, "He's not going to cut in on *me*!"?

At many city intersections there is an arrow signal for the right- or left-turn lane. Out-of-town drivers who wish to continue straight on often get caught in these lanes, not realizing that when the arrow appears they will prevent drivers behind them from turning. This can't be helped. But when you're not a stranger and you do know the signal system, do you stay in the through lanes, leaving the right or left sides for those who wish to make the turn?

Many accidents occur, either directly or indirectly, when one car is passing another. When you are doing the passing, do you wait for the right moment and then cut out quickly and move back in as soon as you are a safe distance ahead? And more important, when you are being passed, do you keep to the same speed you've been going, or even slow down, rather than make a race of it? You may feel the urge to speed up when a car is passing you, but two cars, side by side, going faster and faster, cause a very danger-ous situation. This is something that everyone, adult as well as teen-ager, has to watch.

Those rule books I mentioned all talk about not starting up too fast or "dragging" at traffic lights, but few of them discuss dawdling. Nothing is more irritating to the fifth or sixth car stopped at a red light than to have the lead car delay starting. The driver at the rear is immediately convinced he'll never make it, and the beast in him takes over—honking, swearing, or even pulling out of line to avoid another wait. If you're at the head of the line, do you watch for the light to change and start up promptly and smoothly?

"Tailgating" (following too closely behind the car in front of you) is against the law in some states, where the minimum distance that must be left between two cars is clearly specified. But, whether it is in the law books or not, it's a discourteous, uncomfortable habit. It makes the driver in front nervous, it blocks the view in his rear-view mirror somewhat, and it is, of course, just plain dangerous in case of a sudden stop. The average guideline for a safe distance at which to follow another car is to divide your speed by ten, and leave that number of car lengths between you and the car in front. Obviously you can't measure accurately and at times this would seem an exaggerated amount, but it's not a bad rule of thumb.

I'm sure you've met up with the driver who suddenly cuts across one or two lanes of traffic to make a turn, or to get to the exit off a thruway. If he had thought ahead, he surely would have moved slowly into the right lane when there was a break in the traffic, rather than having to make his move in a hurry, regardless of the cars he cuts off. When you see the "Exit 12, one mile ahead" sign, do you start edging your way over so that you'll be in the right lane well before you have to make your turn?

Let's say you're driving along a two-lane country road at thirty-five or forty miles per hour. Maybe your jalopy won't go any faster, maybe you and your date are having a serious talk, or maybe you're just enjoying the scenery. Whatever the reason, you look in your mirror and see that eight cars have piled up behind you. They can't pass, because the road is narrow and winding, so what do you do? Would you, since you're in no hurry, pull off the road at a safe spot and let them go by? Truck drivers often do this, and I've been stuck behind many motorists who could take a lesson from them.

Your horn is, in a way, your voice when you're driving. Few boys would stand at the curb and yell for their girls to come out, yet they'll park in the street and honk the horn. Most people wouldn't shout at pedestrians who are crossing the street to "step on it," but many will use their horns to say the same thing. A little "beep" to say hello to a passing friend and to attract his attention is perfectly all right, but a prolonged blast will cause everyone around to jump. When you're behind the wheel, do you use your horn with restraint—as a polite warning—in the way it was intended to be used?

## Parking Politeness

This has relatively little to do with safety, but it has to do with courtesy and it's important. Your parking manners are an indication of your manners in every other phase of automobile driving. In parking lots, or when parking on the street, do you make a real effort to stay within the lines—to take up one space only? When you're parked parallel to the curb, and there are cars behind and in front of you, do you leave space for both so that you don't trap either of them? Finally, when you see a car ahead of you stop, preparatory to backing into a space, do you stop well behind, giving him plenty of space to maneuver? The unpardonable sin, of course, is to sneak in frontward and steal his space, but I won't even imply that you might do that.

## Thoughts for Passengers

All the above suggestions are directly related to drivers and driving. But a passenger also has obligations. By exercising a little thoughtfulness, a rider can make life much pleasanter for everyone else in the car and can actually boost safety factors too.

For example, if you're a girl, seated next to the driver, do you expect him to light your cigarette? I hope not. To give you a light, he not only has to take his hands off the wheel, but his eyes off the road. The shoe is really on the other foot—the passenger should light the driver's cigarette, letting him keep his full attention on his driving.

Another gesture, which is good for exactly the same reason, is for a passenger to have change ready before the car reaches a toll booth. If he doesn't have exact change, he should warn the driver, so that they are not stuck in the wrong lane when it may be dangerously late to switch.

Seating arrangements can sometimes be confusing. On a double date, when the nondriver's date is picked up first, does she get into the back seat then and there so that she won't have to climb out and in again when the driver's girl arrives? Not on your life. Any teen-ager who doesn't have the pep to climb in and out of the car a few times doesn't deserve to have a date, and it's pretty unfriendly to leave the driver up front by himself, looking like Joe Chauffeur

If the couple in back want to be as close as Siamese twins, they should have the sense to sit to one side. Remember that two heads glued together are awfully difficult to see around when they're in the center of the rear-view mirror.

Here's a note especially for the boys. When there is a girl in the back seat, open the small front-vent window instead of, or in addition to, the big one. It's a rare girl indeed who doesn't object to a gale blowing violently on the hair she spent all afternoon setting.

The old-fashioned gesture of holding the car door for a date is just as nice as it ever was. No sensible girl will sit indefinitely waiting for someone to open a door for her, but if he does it before she gets impatient, you can be sure she'll be pleased. That old saying I like so much fits well here—"Good manners should always be expected, but never demanded." However, when the car is parked on a crowded street, the boy should not risk his life, or take the chance of causing an accident, by helping his girl in from the curb and then going around to the street side to get in. In a driveway, certainly; but on a busy street, Jim slides in and lets Sally follow.

# 17 Your Mealtime Manners

Throughout most of this chapter on table manners, I'm going to assume that we follow exactly the same rules at home as we do at a dinner party or in a restaurant. I realize, of course, that few of us are as careful within the bosoms of our families as we ought to be, but our standards should never be allowed to slip too low. If we don't make an effort at home, our bad habits will invariably show up in public. Rules about eating have evolved over a long period of time and have been laid down for three sensible reasons: first, to make eating inoffensive to other people; second, to create as little mess as possible; and third, to provide everyone with a guide to the most practical and simplest way of handling food. Eating is great fun, but it can be physically unattractive unless we follow a few simple rules—rules that make mealtimes much more pleasurable. Dinnertime is usually the one hour of the day when the family gets together socially, and so it should never be a time of nagging and scolding. This chapter may sound like an awful lot of "dos" and "don'ts," and you probably know most of them already. But you may find some new and useful suggestions, and my intention is to help you feel more confident of your table manners so that you can enjoy more than ever one of life's greatest pleasures—good food!

I'm going to start from the beginning of dinnertime and go right through the meal, trying to discuss all the situations that might give rise to a question or stump you at any time, anywhere.

When *dinner is announced,* either by your mother from the kitchen, or the hostess or maid at a formal dinner party, move promptly. When a soufflé is ready, it's ready, and no cook will appreciate your dawdling around until it collapses.

At a dinner party, a boy should *hold the chair* for the girl on his right; at home whoever sits on your mother's left should seat her. If she's in the kitchen when everyone gets to the table, it's all right to sit down, but the boys should stand up when she comes in. In a big family, teen-agers should take turns helping to serve dinner and to clear the table. Washing-up arrangements are up to your mother, but I believe that everyone should pitch in.

A *napkin* is unfolded and put in your lap without being shaken out like a dust cloth. At the end of the meal, it is folded and put in a napkin ring if you use one, or laid at the right side of your place in loose folds, not in a crumpled ball. When you're dining out, wait for your hostess to put her napkin on the table (her signal that it's time to leave the table) before placing your own there. Napkins are used like a blotter, somewhat delicately—not as a washcloth to scrub your face.

If *grace* is said before meals in your home, you know what to do; but in case you are unfamiliar with the custom, simply sit still with your head slightly bowed until the prayer is finished.

*Posture* at the table is a dead giveaway of a person's age and *savoir-faire*. Slouching, squirming, or—to the horror of the hostess—tipping back in a chair, doesn't make you an attractive dinner guest. Drawing on the tablecloth with your fork, fiddling with your glass, etc., are signs of either nervousness or boredom. Sit at a comfortable distance from the table—not so close that you can't take a deep breath. While you're waiting to be served, you may clasp your hands and rest your elbows, not your entire forearms, on the table. But arms and elbows come off the table when eating begins.

It's all right to *reach* for the salt and pepper as long as you don't stretch across your neighbor. If something is too far away, simply ask the nearest person to it, "Would you please pass the jelly, Joe?"

When *serving yourself* with two utensils from a platter or vegetable dish, lift the food with the spoon and use the fork to steady it. Replace the spoon and fork on the platter side by side, far enough on it so that there is no danger of their toppling off. If the food is something that's served on toast, such as creamed mushrooms, asparagus, or sweetbreads, slide the spoon under the toast and lift the whole portion carefully—even though you may not wish to eat the toast.

Among friends you may refuse a dish you dislike—or which dislikes you—with a polite "No, thank you." At a formal party, it is better manners to take a very small helping and eat a little of it if you possibly can. It is not necessary to eat every bit of food on your plate.

*Gravy* is served with a spoon, not poured from the gravy boat. It is put right over meat and potatoes or rice; other accompaniments, such as jelly or relish, are placed beside the food they go with.

*Olives, radishes, celery* are put on the butter plate if there is one; otherwise they are put on the edge of your dinner plate.

When serving dishes are passed around the table *"family style,"* set them down on your left, help yourself, and then pass them on. If the table is crowded, the person preceding you may offer to hold the dish for you; then you do the same for the next in line. Otherwise, just hold the dish in your left hand and serve yourself with your right as best you can.

In passing your plate to the head of the table for a *second helping,* leave the knife and fork on it, but be sure they are secure.

At a large party you may *start eating* after three or four guests have been served. The hostess should say, "Please start or your dinner will get cold," but, if she forgets, pick up your fork and others will follow suit. In a group of four or six, it is certainly more polite to wait for everyone. At a family meal, if Dad is delayed by carving the roast or Mom has a last-minute chore in the kitchen, ask permission to begin.

*"How do I know which fork to use?"* The answer is so simple. You start with the implement farthest away from your plate. Of course, if the little shellfish fork has been placed next to your plate, you wouldn't use the dinner fork for your shrimp cocktail; but, in general, you may assume that the silver is in the correct order for each course, and you simply work from the outside in.

Some *desserts* are eaten with your spoon, others with your fork; and occasionally both implements are used. Stewed fruits, custards, ice cream, or "runny" desserts require a spoon. Cake, pastry, or pie is eaten with a fork. If the pie is *à la mode,* the spoon may be used, too, for the ice cream.

A small piece of bread makes a perfectly acceptable "pusher." If you have no bread, your knife may be used: hold it in your left hand and guide the food onto the fork.

Goblets or *glasses with stems* should be held by the bowl; otherwise it becomes a balancing act to get them to your mouth without spilling.

Eat as much of the meat as you can from *olive and fruit pits* and remove them from your mouth with your fingers. Stewed-fruit pits are eaten clean, dropped into your spoon held close to your mouth, and then are put on the edge of your plate.

If, in spite of your best efforts, you *spill* some jelly or squirt the peas off your plate, use the blade of a clean knife to pick up the jelly, or a clean spoon to catch the peas. Don't try to do it with your fingers! If your glass of water tips over, run for a sponge or cloth at home, but in a restaurant call the waiter. Unless it is running all over you or your neighbor, don't try to sop it up with your napkin.

## Difficult Foods

I'm not going to bore you with instructions on how to manage a large number of "difficult" foods, but there are a certain few about which I receive so many questions that it seems wise to tell you how to cope with them.

Salad *may* be cut with your knife if you wish to. If a salad knife isn't provided, use your dinner knife. Cutting lettuce into a reasonable mouthful is certainly more practical than folding it up into a precarious, springy package!

Raw fruit such as apples or pears should be cut into quarters and the core removed before the fruit is eaten with the fingers.

Artichoke leaves are eaten with the fingers. They are pulled off one at a time, dipped in the sauce, and the edible portion is bitten off. The "choke" which remains on the heart when the leaves are gone is scraped away with your knife and the heart is eaten with your knife and fork.

Asparagus is traditionally eaten with the fingers but I'm against it. The limp, buttery stalk is not very attractive waving in the air, so it should be cut and eaten like any other vegetable.

Corn on the cob is a stickler, and the best you can do is attack it with as little ferocity as possible. Butter and eat only two or three rows at a time so that you don't have the whole greasy ear smearing your hands and face. Use holders in each end if they are provided; otherwise, corn is strictly a finger food.

Chicken and chop bones may be picked up only when you're at an informal affair. Do it as neatly as possible after you've cut off as much meat as possible, and wipe your hands and mouth after each bite.

Shrimp cocktail is difficult if the shrimp are jumbo—too big to be eaten in one bite. When they are served in a glass with a stem, knives are not permissible because the glass is apt to tip over. You just have to do your best with the edge of your fork, with a *firm* grip on the shrimp cup with the other hand. When they are served in a stemless bowl or on a plate, you may use your knife to cut them.

Spaghetti is considered an Italian dish and should be eaten as the Italians eat it. A few strands are held against the edge of the plate with the end of the fork, which is then twisted to wrap the spaghetti around the tines. When you have a nice neat coil, get as much to your mouth as possible and bite off the trailers. Don't suck up the ends with a loud slurp!

Soup is sometimes served in a cup with one or two handles. The cup may be picked up if the soup is cool enough to drink, or you may use the spoon. When it is served in a soup plate, tip the plate away from you to get the last spoonfuls. Blowing on soup to cool it invariably results in a mess, so let nature take its course, without the aid of a cooling breeze.

Crisp bacon, bite-size portions of baked-potato skins, watermelon, and pickles are all eaten from the fingers, as well as the obvious foods—sandwiches, corn on the cob, etc. But éclairs or napoleons, whose fillings squirt when they're squeezed, and cake with soft icing, must be tackled with a fork.

Bread and rolls are broken into two or three pieces. To butter them, hold the pieces close to the plate in your fingers—not flat on the palm of your hand! If you want to sop up your gravy, that's fine, but do it by breaking bite-size pieces of bread into the gravy or sauce and using your fork to eat them.

## The Most Important Don'ts

Don't take a drink of anything when you already have a mouthful of food.

Don't wipe off silverware or your glass in a restaurant. If something isn't clean, ask for a replacement.

Don't spread jam or jelly directly from the serving dish. With the spoon provided, put a little on your plate first, and use your knife to spread it. If there is no spoon, use the knife to serve it, too.

Don't ever leave your spoon in your cup, or in a cereal or dessert bowl. Or the fork in a shrimp cup. They belong on the saucer or plate underneath.

Don't overload your fork—in other words, take moderate-sized mouthfuls.

Need I say it? Don't talk with your mouth full!

Don't suck ice cream off your spoon in little bits. Put on the spoon only the amount that can be eaten all at once.

Don't push your plate away when you're finished. At home, wait until everyone else has finished; if you're in a hurry and you've been excused, take the plate to the kitchen. When you're dining out, leave your dish where it is.

Don't pick up lump sugar or ice with your fingers when a serving implement is provided.

Don't cut all the food on your plate at once; cut a bite or two at a time.

Don't spit a fish bone or anything inedible into your napkin. As unobtrusively as possible, slip it out of your mouth and onto your fork, or into your fingers if it's relatively dry, and then put it on the edge of your plate.

Don't serve anything with an implement that has been used—for instance your used coffee spoon does not go back into the bowl to get more sugar when your coffee isn't sweet enough. If there is no sugar spoon, ask for, or at home go and get, a clean spoon for the bowl.

Don't smoke at the table unless the presence of an ash tray at your place makes it obvious that the hostess approves.

For girls only—don't wear excessive lipstick to the table. Consider your hostess's napkin and the appearance of the red smear on the edge of your glass.

# 18 Full- and Part-time Jobs

## How Do I Begin?

Job hunting is a serious business—a very practical matter. Therefore, I'm going to be very practical about it and start exactly where you'll be starting. First, consider your qualifications carefully.

1. Do you like to handle telephone calls, file, type, keep accounts? If so, consider an office job.
2. Do you like meeting people? This is the first requisite for a successful sales person.
3. Are you slim and gorgeous? Then you may be one of the few who can "make it" in modeling.

4. Are you basically the athletic type? Try for a job as an assistant athletic teacher, camp counselor, etc.
5. Are you artistic? Try museums, art galleries, art schools, and advertising agencies.

In other words, don't be a square peg in a round hole. No one is ever successful at a job he hates; insofar as your ability permits, choose a field in which you think you'll be happy. Second, start to look for a job through the following channels:

1. Talk to your parents—they know you best and will have helpful ideas about what you'll enjoy and be capable of doing. Your father may be able to put you in touch with prospective employers through business contacts or friends. Don't scorn this sort of "pull." In the business world it's every man for himself and you are free to use any honest help you can get. And give thanks for it!
2. Go to your school or college guidance office. They are experienced with young people and part of their job is to help job hunters.
3. Check the classified advertisements in your local newspaper. Large companies as well as private individuals often prefer to find their employees in this way. Also, from the openings listed by employment agencies, you can frequently tell which ones handle the sort of job you're looking for.
4. Try your local employment agencies. There are advantages and disadvantages to this. You have to pay a fee, of course, if you get a job through their offices—usually a substantial sum. On the other hand, they can tell you something about the company offering the position, and what your chances are.

Finally, prepare a résumé—a history of yourself. This should include:

Name, address, telephone number, age.
Schools attended, grades completed.
Diplomas or certificates received.
Courses related to the job you're applying for.
Interests and hobbies, if pertinent to the position you're seeking.

Past working experience, if any.
Give the names and addresses of at least three persons from among:
  Previous employers
  Clergymen
  Teachers
  Family friends
    who would be willing to provide references. Family friends
    should be notified that they may receive such a request.

Take the direct approach. Many people have landed jobs by
simply walking into a store or office, asking for the personnel director, and then convincing him that the applicant is the one he
needs to fill an opening. This takes more nerve than some of the
other approaches, but it may result in an instant job.

Prepare yourself in advance. You will probably start to think
about getting a job some time before the actual day arrives to do
so. If it's an office job you want, take a typing course. In fact, I
firmly believe that *everyone* should know how to type. There are
very few positions which do not at some time require a certain
amount of typing, and many companies do not even consider an
applicant who cannot type at least thirty words a minute. If newspaper work appeals to you, take some writing or journalism
courses; if it's the art world, study history of art or whatever
aspect of the field most interests you. In short, don't arrive at your
interview and say, "Well, I haven't studied that, but I plan to take
some courses." Do it in advance!

## Your First Interview

With all the preliminaries out of the way, you're ready to face your
first interview. The appointment may be made by telephone or by
letter, but, whichever way you make it, be sure that you have the
address, the name of the interviewer, and the hour correct—and
*don't be late!* When you arrive, go directly to the receptionist or
secretary, tell her your name, and at what hour you have an appointment with Mr. Personnel. Then sit down and wait patiently
until she tells you to go in.

The first thing an employer will take note of is, of course, your

appearance. It is not the elegance of your clothes and grooming that will count, but rather their neatness and appropriateness. Your hair should be clean and combed, your hands and nails immaculate, your clothes spotless, pressed, and conservative in style, and, if you're a girl, your make-up restrained. Medium heels rather than spikes, a good-looking suit or tailored dress rather than a skin-tight knit, and a simple hairdo instead of a teased tower add up to a well-groomed working girl. A boy makes the best impression dressed in slacks or trousers—not jeans—a shirt and tie, well-shined shoes or loafers, and a conservative sports jacket. If it's a job in a bank or business office, a suit is always appropriate. Your manner should not, of course, be bold, but neither should you be timid. Modesty combined with self-confidence makes the ideal combination.

Let your interviewer direct the conversation, but when he turns the lead over to you be ready with some intelligent questions as to the training program, opportunities for advancement, and the work you would be doing. You may certainly ask about details of vacation time, pay, and so forth, but *after* you have established the fact that you are interested in the work itself. The interviewer will undoubtedly ask you why you want to work for the XYZ Company and what your expectations are, as well as about your training and past experience. Have your answers ready. Nothing makes a better impression than a quick, intelligent reply as opposed to a floundering "Well, er, um, I really don't know." Answer all questions as fully as you can, but don't ramble. The interviewer probably has other applicants to see.

If you are asked to take some tests, don't panic. Experienced personnel managers allow for the fact that you are somewhat nervous. Answer as many questions as you can, rather than wasting minutes over one that stumps you, and, above all, read the questions and instructions carefully. Following them to the letter is often more important than the answers you give. The same holds true for filling out application blanks: take care to answer all the questions.

Remember your good manners. A polite greeting, a thank-you when you leave, and calling the interviewer by his name all help to make you look better than average. Don't chew gum, don't smoke, and don't sit down until you're asked to.

Even though there may be several jobs open, don't go with a group to apply. Right after graduation time, personnel departments are swamped with applications, and if you want to stand out from the crowd, you would be wise to call a week or two before school ends and make an appointment for yourself alone. You'll make more of an impression this way. A nice final touch is to write a short note afterward, thanking the interviewer for his kindness.

The interviewer will probably tell you what the starting salary will be, but occasionally he may turn the tables on you and ask how much you think you should be paid. Be prepared for this. Discuss it in advance with your parents or friends who have held similar jobs, or your school guidance counselor. It will give you an edge over other applicants if you are knowledgeable about the going rates; nine out of ten will answer, "I don't know."

If by any chance the job is offered to you on the spot, it's a good idea to give yourself a few hours to think it over. Of course, if you're absolutely sure it's exactly what you want, accept it then and there. But if you want to discuss it with your family, or think over the information you have received, don't hesitate to say politely, "Thank you so much. May I let you know tomorrow morning?" It's more probable that the interviewer will say, "You'll hear from us next week," and, if he does, don't try to pin him down any further. Smile, thank him for his kindness, and tell him you'll be waiting to hear from him. Even though he may not have a place for you immediately, if your manners, attitude, and appearance make a good impression, he will remember you the next time there is an opening. If, before you hear from him, you decide to take another job, write or call immediately to tell him so that he can consider other applicants.

It's never as hard to be interviewed as you imagine it will be, and the friendlier your manner, the more enthusiastic will be the response.

## Successful Sitters

Chances are that the first job a teen-age girl will hold is that of babysitter. And boys, too, are finding this an easy and practical way to make money. Sitting in the evening doesn't interfere with school, with sports, with after-school recreation, or with homework —what could be more ideal?

A really good, reliable babysitter is in such demand that she can be just as busy as she wishes. There are lots of things to consider if you've never had a sitting job, and many that may not have occurred to you even if you have "sat" occasionally. Never forget, for example, that your first duty is to keep your charges safe, and the second is to keep them contented. I'm going to make some suggestions that should not only make your job more fun, but should result in more money in the bank.

After you have been a sitter for a family a number of times you will know their routine and their regulations. But when you start out on your first job, or go to a home you've never been in before, there is a definite procedure to follow and information about the household that you should learn.

## ESTABLISH YOUR RATES

When the mother calls to ask you to sit, establish your pay rates immediately and clearly. If you expect overtime pay when parents arrive home late, or if you wish to be paid a bonus for extra duties, such as cooking the children's meal, say so. It's terribly unpleasant to get into a hassle over the fee or not to know what to say when the parents ask how much they owe you at the end of the evening.

## START OUT RIGHT

If you don't know the children, ask if you may arrive a few minutes early to get acquainted while the parents are still at home. It will smooth over possible difficulties if small children realize that you and their mother and father are all in the same league.

You'll make an immediate hit with the youngsters if you spend the first few minutes entertaining them. Read to them, play games, do a few card tricks, or make them something out of paper or string. Don't rush them off to bed too fast just so you can see your favorite TV show. Let them sit up with you and make their after-supper hour fun.

## BE FIRM, NOT FURIOUS

Be firm about eating, bedtime hours, and any other regulations the parents have made—but never, never strike a child. Some parents do believe in spanking, others don't; in any case, it is *not* up to a sitter to discipline in this way. You may deprive them of TV, you may call off games or reading, or you may send them to bed early, but you must not punish in any more severe form.

LIST IMPORTANT INFORMATION

If you plan to make sitting a regular job, you should have a list of questions to ask the parents when you arrive. It can be a mental list, but it's better to make it a written one, because not only are you apt to forget some of the things you wanted to know, but you're almost sure to forget some of the answers. A good list would include:

*Feeding Instructions:*
What food; is it ready or to be prepared?
At what time do the children eat?
How much *must* they finish?
Any special table rules?
*Bedtime:*
What time?
Light left on, door open, etc.?
How many trips for water or bathroom?
Baby picked up if he cries?
Bath necessary?
*TV and Radio:*
Instructions on use.
*Telephone:*
Limitations on use?
*General Questions:*
Do parents object if you nap when they expect to be very late?
If not, where?
May your girl friend come over to keep you company? (Needless to say—no boys.)
What snacks or drinks may you take?
Instructions for using dishwasher; for instance, are there any things that may not be put in it?
If employers are not taking you home, and you cannot arrange for transportation, what arrangements can be made? For example, will the employer pay for a taxi?

Make a form out of as much or as little as you wish of the preceding list, but you *must* write down *two* numbers, and put them close to the phone—the number where the parents can be reached, and the number of the children's doctor. With these two numbers, and the possibility of calling your own parents in an emergency, you should be able to cope with any situation.

### NEVER LET AN EMPLOYER DOWN

There are two last points to remember. First, never let an employer down. If you cannot possibly keep a date, do your level best to find a replacement. It may be that every reliable person you know is busy that night; if so, call the parents far enough in advance so that they themselves can find a substitute.

### ADMIT YOUR ERRORS

Second, last, and very important—don't be afraid to admit to the parents any troubles you may have had. It is their right to know if the children are misbehaving in their absence. It is also their right to know of any mistakes *you* may have made. Older people realize that teen-agers learn by experience, and they admire those who admit their errors and want to learn from them. Frankness will win you many more jobs than a smooth "Oh, everything went beautifully," when the evening was really a chamber of horrors!

## Girls in Office Jobs

You've actually landed your job! The day to start has arrived. The first day on any job, but most especially the very first job, is one of the scariest, most confusing, loneliest, most exciting experiences you can have. You feel like an idiot. You don't know whom to go to for what, which faces belong to the names you hear, where to find even the most basic essentials, and, probably, how to begin your work.

### THE FIRST DAY

If you can remember that everyone *knows* you're new, and no one *expects* you to absorb all the hows, whos, and whats in the first day, you will get through that hard time much more easily. Ask questions when you really need to, not just out of nervousness, and respond with friendliness to any openings the other employees give you. Don't bubble or gush, and don't push. Friendships will come naturally and will be the ones you really want if you restrain your enthusiasm until you have had a little longer acquaintance. Susie at the next desk may look like a perfect doll, but turn out to be a real witch when you know her better. If you have rushed pell-mell into a quick friendship with her, it is sometimes very difficult to extricate yourself without embarrassment and hurt feelings.

YOUR ATTITUDE

Even more important than your skill at your specific work—although I certainly don't mean to underrate that—is your attitude toward your job. Ask yourself the following questions and, if you can't honestly and unreservedly answer "yes" to every one of them, you should take a good look at whether you're earning your keep.

Can you truly say that you are *not* "on the make" for your boss or other male employees?

Do you firmly refuse to discuss your boss, your fellow workers, and your company's private business with outsiders?

Do you avoid gossiping with co-workers?

Do you leave your personal problems at home?

Would you, without grumbling, do any out-of-the-ordinary work your boss might need in a hurry?

Would you give a few extra minutes of your time to finish up a job after closing time?

Do you take an interest in the appearance of the office?

Do you try to keep a smile on your face, no matter how black a mood it's hiding?

ACCURACY

It's hard for most of us who haven't worked in an office to recognize the importance of accuracy. It *is* important, and lack of it is one of the main causes of criticism frequently aimed at young employees. The addition or subtraction of one zero to a figure can cost a company an enormous amount of money. Neglecting to write down a telephone message may result in the loss of a sale, and taking a phone number inaccurately can cause endless delay and irritation.

If your job requires shorthand, be sure that you can read your own notes. It's awfully annoying to an executive if a girl constantly comes in and says, "What was the word after 'dividend,' Mr. Bankhead? I can't seem to read what I have here." Another frustration to a busy man is poor typing. It's better to slow down, check your spelling, and perfect the appearance of your letters than to have them sent back time and again to be retyped because of hasty and careless errors.

## PROMPTNESS

Promptness isn't only arriving at your office on (or before) the dot; it's also answering the phone before the ringing drives everyone wild, and responding to your superior's call or buzzer before he's gnashing his teeth.

Don't cheat on lunch hours. Your hours will undoubtedly be made very clear to you, and if your boss leaves at 12:00 and says he won't be back until 2:00, that's no reason for you to feel entitled to the same privilege. You'll be terribly embarrassed the day you come back at 1:55 and find the man fuming because his unexpected arrival at 1:30 caught you still out at lunch.

Coffee breaks are a great institution—within limits. Use them to relax, enjoy them to chat, but don't abuse the privilege by extending them until there is more time-off than time-on.

## BE ORGANIZED

People who keep themselves and their possessions neat are almost always orderly in every way. Look at the girl with uncombed hair and a spotted blouse and then look at her desk. I'd be willing to bet it's a hodge-podge of scattered papers, loaded ash trays, and general clutter. Now look at the girl you've always admired as the neatest, trimmest thing around, and her work area will almost invariably be uncluttered and organized.

There are other habits which are worth cultivating. A few are:

Clearing up your desk before leaving at night.
Emptying your ash tray frequently.
Not leaving empty coffee cups, paper napkins, candy wrappers, etc., on your desk.

If for any reason you cannot possibly get to work, call and let your superior know.

Don't be a pack rat. Keep your desk drawers free of gloves, nail polish, and other accessories, and so organized that you can find things easily and quickly.

Remember that the phone on your desk is not there for your personal use. Although some offices forbid personal calls, most won't object to your making or receiving an occasional one, but keep it short. Your boss *will* object if he finds a client was unable to get through to him because you had the line tied up discussing last night's date.

## Leaving A Job

No matter how much you may dislike your employer or the job you're leaving, give your notice with good grace. This is important, because word gets around, especially in a small town, and the girl who leaves a good impression when she quits her job will have a better recommendation to take to her next prospective employer. Unless it is otherwise specified in an agreement or by company policy, an employee should give two weeks' notice in order to give the company time to find a replacement.

## Retail Jobs

So many boys and girls take summer or after-school jobs in stores that I'd like to offer a few suggestions that could lead to a raise or even a promotion.

Know your products and where to find them. It doesn't matter if it's a supermarket or a five-and-dime; when a customer asks, "Where can I find the cereal," or "the nail polish," or "parakeet food," you should be able to give the information instantly. Your supervisor won't appreciate having to stop to tell you where it is, and the customer doesn't want to wait while you go to hunt it down.

Don't stick to other teen-age workers like a gaggle of geese. It's almost inevitable, if you do, that you'll start to joke and gab, and that's not getting your job done.

As in all jobs, be neat and dress appropriately. Flat heels on girls may not look as glamorous as high ones, but at the end of the day you'll be walking a lot more gracefully than if your feet are killing you. Boys must be guided by what their employers want them to wear, but cleanliness and neatness are essential in every customer-contact job.

An attitude of boredom must definitely be avoided. The half-asleep, gum-chewing salesman or salesgirl, leaning wearily on a counter, discourages the customer before he even starts to make a purchase. In a lull between sales, rearrange and straighten stock, check accounts, or whatever—but do something, *anything,* to keep from looking (and being) bored.

Accuracy is just as important in a store as it is in an office. If you are selling clothing in a retail store, your checks must be made out correctly and legibly, otherwise charges may be put on the wrong account or customers may be grossly over- or undercharged. Many stores have lost good customers through this sort of carelessness.

If your job is at a checkout counter, learn to give change quickly and accurately. Don't ever be afraid to ask questions of older employees. Checks, receipts, charge plates, and cash are all handled in different ways in individual stores, and if your boss neglects to indoctrinate you properly you must count on those who have been there longer to help.

# 19 Sportsmanship and Sports

There's no question about it—being good *at* sports is an asset to any young person. But of far more importance is being a good sport. Not everyone can excel at athletics; some people are naturally more coordinated than others, and there are some who simply aren't interested in active sports. But the number of those who *never* participate in some type of game is few indeed, and sportsmanship is vitally important to all who do—winners as well as losers.

I don't know whether it's harder to be a good winner or a good loser. A young girl asked me on a radio program the other day what she should do when she won a tennis match. The most important thing I could tell her was that no matter by how wide a margin she had won, or how poor a player she considered her opponent, she should try to convince the loser that it had been a good match. If the winner can help the loser to think that he or she has played a good game, and been fun to play against, she has succeeded in being a winner that everyone can applaud. The winner who gives the impression that a match was a bore and not a real contest certainly won't be popular with either opponents or audience.

To be a good loser requires a different approach, and it is really a harder challenge. Swearing at your luck, making excuses, complaining about conditions, and, worst of all, protesting a decision by a referee or umpire gets you nowhere except into trouble. Of course luck can be a factor; but, in general, you lose because on that day you play an inferior game, and the test of a good loser is his being able to accept that loss and act as if he had enjoyed the match and played his best. You must be sincere in your congratulations.

A good sport accepts any turn of events as part of the game, but he doesn't have to be a wooden-faced robot. It's only natural to show a little elation when a long putt drops into the hole or your doubles partner aces your opponents. What you must *never* do is show the same elation when anyone playing against you makes an error.

Comments like "Gee, that's a shame—a perfect split!" at the bowling alley, or "Too bad, just an inch out!" on the tennis court have a distinct note of gloating and your opponent knows it!

It isn't necessary to discuss sportsmanship in team play because your coach and the other members of the team will take care of that in a hurry. But there are certain regulations in every game you play as an individual that are essential for the pleasure of others involved and for your own enjoyment. So many sports are played in various parts of the country that it would be impossible to consider each and every one. But, no matter which one, or ones, you enjoy, you will have a better time and be more in demand as a partner or opponent if you show consideration, enthusiasm, and good sportsmanship.

## Sailing

If you're lucky enough to be asked to cruise with an even luckier friend who has a sailboat of his own, you and your host will enjoy it more if you follow these suggestions:

Take as little clothing as possible. Even if it's a long cruise with a number of trips ashore planned, remember that one or two dresses for a girl and one jacket for a boy will do—after all, the people in Sandy Point will not have seen you in your red dress the night before in Rockport. Drip-dry materials are best—you can sometimes rinse out, but you can't iron!

Ask your host if he has extra foul-weather gear; if not, borrow or buy your own.

Hard-soled shoes are both unpopular and dangerous on a boat. They damage decks and they are slippery. Stick to rubber or fiber soles or bare feet.

Squashable canvas duffel bags or sacks are essential. Hard suitcases are space-consuming and difficult to stow.

Because of the limited space on a boat, you must be neater than you've ever been in your life; there just isn't any room for litter!

On a boat which carries a paid captain, he is treated with friendliness and respect but not intimacy. His quarters are separate, and he generally eats his meals apart from the guests. You do not tip him.

Remember to toss tossable items to leeward. If you throw cigarettes or matches or the dregs from your coffee cup to windward, you'll probably either burn or soak the deck, yourself, and the other sailors.

Even more than your host at a house party on shore, the skipper is absolute boss on board, and his word goes. Don't try to help unless he asks you to, but if he does do your job quickly and enthusiastically. If you don't know what he's talking about when he says, "Grab that sheet!" ask him, rather than looking desperately for the bedding.

Take along something for the boat or a contribution to the food or drink supply, just as you would take a gift to a host or hostess when you visit on land.

## Tennis Playing

The rules of sportsmanship are terribly important in tennis. There are only two or four players on the court and your manners are really on display.

Follow the rules of your club or community as to clothing. White shorts or dresses are often required, and sneakers, invariably. Bare feet are definitely not the thing on the tennis court.

Never, never question the ruling of a linesman or the referee. He won't change his decision anyway, and it makes you look like a poor sport.

When your ball goes into the next court, wait until the players there have finished their point before asking for, or retrieving, it.

If the sun or wind favors your side of the court, offer to change sides on every odd game.

Even though your courts may have no regulations, avoid signing up to play on weekends, which are the only times your fathers have a chance. Try to get your tennis in during the week.

If the court you have signed for is still occupied when you arrive, wait patiently a few minutes for the players to finish. On the other hand, if you're the one still playing, don't try to finish the match unless you're within a few points of ending it. Completing the game you're in should be the limit.

Don't try to hop over the net at the end of the match just because they do it in the movies. It's apt to be a disaster, and a handshake is just as effective.

If you're making a lot of errors, don't keep apologizing to your partner. After the first few bad shots, one "I'm sorry, Joe, I seem to be off my game today" is plenty!

A sincere "Good shot!" when your opponent makes one puts you way ahead in the sportsmanship race.

In a friendly game without a referee, insist on playing over any point that is questioned.

## Skiing

Most of the rules of etiquette for skiers are concerned with safety as well as manners. Therefore, they are even more important to observe than those in many other sports.

If you're a novice, don't ski the "expert" trails. Not only will you very possibly break a leg, but you'll infuriate the experts who belong there. They can hardly appreciate it when they whip around a bend in the trail and find a beginner nervously snowplowing down ahead of them.

On the other hand, if you're the expert, don't scare the novices out of their wits by hurtling down the beginners' slopes.

When you overtake another skier on a trail, call, "Track right," if you intend to pass on his right, or "Track left" for the other side. This will warn him against turning into you as you pass.

If you do have a collision and knock someone down, stop, apologize, and make sure he is all right. If he isn't, don't try to move him, but get to the nearest ski patrol as fast as you can. If there are other skiers around, have someone stay with the injured person, or stay yourself and ask the others to go for help.

Don't shove in ahead of others in the tow line, don't swing the lift chairs, and don't kick off your skis and leave them any old way in front of the lodge. Racks are provided for them.

## Golf

Golfing etiquette, like skiing etiquette, is designed partly to insure safety on the course. If there were no rules about waiting until players were out of range, or the correct way to "go through," can you imagine the mayhem that would result?

Don't play golf if you can't keep your temper! No other game strains one's self-control as golf does, and it's not worth the criticism you'll get from young and old alike if you let your emotions get out of hand. Those who throw clubs and slam them into the green or fairway (and this isn't a sin confined to youth—I've seen octogenarians do it!) are not appreciated by greenskeepers. And those who swear, blame the course, and sulk when they're losing aren't popular with other players.

Never hit your shot until the group ahead is well out of range. Before driving, wait until the foursome in front of you have at least all hit their second shots.

Never play a blind shot (when you can't see the area you expect your ball to land in) without a caddy or another player going ahead to make sure there is no one within range.

If a wild shot is heading toward another player, yell "Fore" at the top of your lungs; he just may have time to put his arms over his head.

Don't take practice swings when you are near enough to other players to scare them, let alone hit them, or spray them with dirt.

Never talk or move while other players are making their shots. You may think they can't hear or see you, but it's amazing how much one catches from the corner of his eye when he's concentrating on the ball.

Be ready to play when your turn comes. Nothing slows up play on the course more than people who have been gabbing while waiting their turns, when they could have been planning what club to use and lining up their shots.

Always let a faster group "go through." You'll enjoy it more, anyway, if they aren't breathing down your neck on every shot. Don't try to go through yourself, though, unless there is one empty hole in front of the players ahead of you. If you are unable to keep moving, it can back up the entire course.

Divots (chunks of turf dug up by your club) must be replaced. It's hard to understand why so many people, who presumably enjoy the game, seem to care so little about keeping the course in good condition.

Avoid walking on greens except when you're putting.

After making a shot out of a trap, be sure that the sand is raked smooth, either by you or a caddy. If you've ever landed in someone's unraked heel print, you know why!

The person farthest away from the hole putts first and continues to putt until he holes out.

Help other members of your foursome look for their balls, and ask the following group to go through if you think the search will delay your group more than a few minutes.

The player who has won the preceding hole drives first on the next, and, if the group tied, whoever won the hole before that one keeps the "honor" of driving first.

Follow these rules, and the local rules which almost every club prints on its score cards, and you'll have a lot of fun on the golf course. You will also find that you'll be welcome there. Whereas the thoughtlessness of teen-agers in some areas has caused membership to bar the use of the course to them, every older player enjoys and welcomes the presence of considerate and careful young players.

## Bowling

More people take up bowling every day, and you'll find that many hours are set aside for adults and team matches. Even at other times, you'll be wise, and save yourself a lot of irritation, if you reserve an alley in advance.

As in every sport where people perform individually, those waiting their turns stay still and quiet while the others take their turns.

Avoid bowling at exactly the same moment as the bowler to the right or left—it's distracting to both of you.

Don't help yourself to someone else's personal ball—any more than you would take someone else's tennis racquet from a locker.

Bowling shoes are required at almost every alley; don't try to get away with sneakers or loafers.

Applying a little "body English" to get that last pin down is O.K., but don't go into contortions and gyrations while your ball is on its way.

As in the case of tennis courts, allow the players still on the alley you've reserved a few minutes to finish their game, and give those that follow you equal consideration by speeding up your last few bowls to clear the alley for them.

## Swimming

The tremendous recent increase in the number of swimming pools has brought with it problems which never existed before. Such knotty questions as:

"Who uses the pool on weekends?"

"How many kids can come over at one time?" and "When may I have them?"

"Do I have to have drinks or snacks for all my friends who come for a dip?"

"Must I provide towels for guests?"

"Are nighttime swimming parties allowed?"

can develop into real sticklers. The sensible thing to do is sit down with your parents when your first pool season starts and establish a set of rules. Pools are wonderful fun, but they are potentially dangerous too. Unlike a golf course or a ski slope, a pool may be on your property, and you are therefore morally obligated to enforce safety regulations. Furthermore, if an accident should occur, you would not only be subject to tremendous remorse and heartache, but your family might well be in for a severe financial blow in the form of a lawsuit.

Let's take the questions listed above one by one.

During your summer vacation, unless you have a full-time job, you are free to use the pool most of the time. But your father is working all day, and has very little, if any, time to swim, so he and your mother should have either Saturday or Sunday (whichever *they* prefer) to keep the pool for "adults only." The other weekend day should be shared by the whole family, and on that day limit your invitations to a friend or two who can be counted on to fit into the family group.

The number of people you may invite at one time depends somewhat on their ages and their swimming ability. Ordinarily, restrict your guests to four or five, or the area will seem like an amusement park. If you want to have more, you must have a capable adult swimmer on hand to pay attention to lifeguarding. In a big crowd, one swimmer can be missing below the surface for quite a time before his absence is noticed.

Until you are in your late teens, fully grown, and an able swimmer, you should *never* ask guests to swim unless there is an adult swimmer within calling distance. Playing water polo, tag, or any other active game around the pool can result in a head's being bumped on the concrete, and anyone can get a cramp at any time. For the same reasons, you should *never, never* swim alone.

A pool is a real social center in the summer, and if you are lucky enough to have one your parents should not be penalized by having to supply the entire neighborhood with food and drink every day. If you have the same gang over often, explain this and suggest that you *all* take turns in providing snacks.

Keep a supply of extra towels for emergencies, but spread the word that you expect guests to bring their own. Again, your mother shouldn't be burdened with all that extra laundry.

Nighttime swimming parties are great, but you must adhere to certain rules. The pool, as well as the surrounding area, must be well lighted to prevent accidents. As at any party, a chaperone should be on hand in the house or close by, and he or she should put in an occasional appearance. After nine or ten o'clock, the party should move inside for the benefit of the neighbors. Incidentally, they should be alerted beforehand, so that they can prepare themselves for the inevitable racket that accompanies a swimming party. If you're all willing to sit and talk quietly, stop horsing around in the pool, and give up the record player, stay outside. But you'll probably have more fun if you don't have to worry about the neighbors' complaining to your parents, or worse, to the police.

When you're invited to someone else's pool, all you have to do is show the same consideration for their property as you would wish them to show yours. Here are a few suggestions:

Don't litter. Put candy or gum wrappers in a pocket or a pocketbook if you don't see a receptacle for trash.

Girls should wear bathing caps if asked to do so. The reason is valid—wads of hair clog up drains and pumps.

Don't leave wet suits or towels in little heaps in the bathhouse. Stretch them out on hooks or pegs, or ask your host or hostess where to put them.

If you enjoy the use of the pool often, offer to help with the cleaning and poolside pickup.

# DATING DATA

# 20 The Opening Formalities

## Making Contact

When you see someone you think you'd like to date, the first problem is to make contact. This is infinitely simpler for a boy than a girl. He only has to find someone who knows her and who will introduce them; then he can ask to walk her home from school, take her to a snack bar for a Coke, or he can just chat for a while to see if she's as attractive close up as she looked from the other side of the auditorium. Lucky boy! It's all up to him: he can end it right there if she's a disappointment; if she's not, he can call the next day and ask for a date.

If the situation is complicated by the lack of a handy friend—for instance, if the boy has seen this lovely creature sunbathing by the club pool every morning for the last week—he still has the advantage. Catching her eye, he can give a friendly smile, then possibly ask her what she's reading, or whether she's joined the club or is just visiting. He'll soon find out whether or not she wants to strike up a friendship. If she gives him a stony look, or answers in monosyllables, he can forget it—her heart is elsewhere. But at least he can make the first move without seeming to press and without being considered obvious, as a girl would who used the same approach.

If a girl doesn't want to appear to be chasing a boy, I'm afraid she has to be more devious. She needn't just sit back and hope, but her efforts must be subtle. Boys are flattered, of course, when someone wants to meet them, but they are often scared by an overzealous attack.

A girl can:

Put on her friendliest smile and say "Hello" whenever their paths cross.

Arrange with a mutual friend to invite them both to a small party.
Go to all school events in which he is either active or interested.
Join school, church, or community organizations of which he is a
 member.
If he likes tennis, bowling, or any other sport, practice up and make
 a good showing on the next court, alley, or whatever.
If possible, get a girl who knows him to arrange a blind (double)
 date.

## Once You've Met

After contact has been made, and it's clear that you'd both like to
see more of each other, the hard part is over and the telephone is
the usual means of asking for a date. But it can just as well be
face to face when you see each other on the street or in school.
However, or wherever, the boy should remember to mention
these details:

What time he'll call for the girl.
If he doesn't drive, the sort of transportation he has arranged.
What kind of date it will be—movies, a school game, a party at a
 friend's house, a dance, a picnic, or other.

If he forgets any of this, the girl may, and *should,* ask him. She
need never feel shy about saying, for example, "Great! I'd love it
—movies, or what?" This produces the information about the sort
of date it will be and the girl will then know what to wear. If her
family wants to know—and they should—what time she'll be home
and who is driving, if the boy is under legal age, this is the moment for the girl to get the answers. Her parents provide the
excuse for asking, and no boy should resent their desire to know
what the plans are.

## Dates Are Usually Made Ahead of Time

Most girls feel insulted when a boy asks for a date at the last
minute. The immediate reaction is that either (a) his original
date fell through and he is desperate, or (b) he thinks the girl is

so unpopular that she'll surely be free and it isn't necessary to call ahead of time. Of course this is not necessarily so, but, generally speaking, a boy should call a girl:

Two to four days ahead for an ordinary date.
At least two weeks ahead for a formal dance.
A month or more ahead for a big college weekend; otherwise she thinks she's "second choice."

Some exceptions—the permissible last-minute invitations—occur when:

A boy and girl are going steady and know the other one will not have another date. They probably know exactly what each other's plans are in any case.
The boy doesn't know in advance whether he'll have sufficient funds.
A party is planned on the spur of the moment.
He is unexpectedly given tickets to a special event.

These exceptions do not apply to a first date; on this occasion the invitation should come at least three days before the date.

## Accepting or Refusing a Date

Accepting a date is no problem unless you're dubious about wanting to go. If that's the case, for your own sake as well as the boy's, put on a good act, and sound as enthusiastic as you can.

If you had been hoping to hear another voice when the phone rang, don't let it show. You must make a quick decision—whether to accept the "bird-in-the-hand" cheerfully, or to wait and hope your true love will call later. The worst mistake you can make is to be evasive. If you really did promise to babysit and don't know if you can get a substitute, or if your mother isn't around and it's a date for which you need permission, say so. But it must be true and you must be sincere, or *he* will know it. Don't ever say, "Can I let you know tomorrow?" without saying why.

Once you have accepted, you must keep that date. The only permissible reasons for breaking it are illness, an unexpected trip, or a family situation that requires your presence. You can *never* break one date to accept another. Should either the jilted man or any of his friends see you, or hear that you were out that night, your name will be mud!

Refusing a date when you'd really like to accept it requires a little tact so that he'll call again. If the reason you must refuse is mentionable, give it—"Oh, John, I'm *so* sorry but we're going to the farm Friday. I'd love to do it some other time." A reason that is true *rings* true and opens the door for him to ask you again.

If you don't want to be that encouraging, all you need do is say, "Bill, I'm awfully sorry but I already have a date for Saturday night." Don't be more specific and you'll be free to accept someone else who calls. If Bill persists, and you honestly want to avoid an entanglement, you must be firm. It's kinder to stop a situation before it starts than to encourage it when you're not interested. If he says, "How about next week?" and the next, and so on, you just have to keep up with him. "Oh, dear, I'm busy then, too." Unless he's terribly thick-skinned, he should get the message, and although he won't like it there'll be no reason for deeply hurt feelings.

Don't make up a specific excuse because you may get stuck with it. If you tell George that you have to stay home for a family get-together, and then Hank, with whom you've been dying to go out, calls—you've had it! You *cannot* appear outside your house that night and trust to luck that George, or George's friends, won't hear about it. A simple refusal, "I'm awfully sorry, I can't do it that night," commits you to nothing and you are free to accept other invitations.

## Introducing Dates to Parents

Unless it's absolutely impossible, a girl should introduce a new friend to her parents on her very first date with him. It makes it a great deal easier for him if, when he arrives at her house, she is ready and opens the door for him herself.

Brief your parents about a boy before he arrives so that they can start the conversation easily. Just take him to the living room, kitchen, or wherever they may be, and say, "Mom and Dad, I'd like you to meet Hank Devon." Allow five or ten minutes of getting-acquainted time, and then make the move to leave by saying, "Hank, we'd better go if we're going to make the start of the movie," or whatever is appropriate.

This little ceremony, as unnecessary as it may seem to you, is very important. It proves to your parents that you want their approval and confidence—that their opinion is important to you—and, what's more, it proves to Hank that you're proud of *him* and want to show him off to your parents.

After you have gone out with Hank a few times, his parents will be eager to meet you too. He may ask you over after dinner some evening when they are home, or he may only want you to stop by at his house and chat with them as he did with your parents. In any case, try not to be silly or self-conscious. Remember that they are just an older couple who would like to make friends with you, so just be your most friendly, natural self.

## Parental Approval

The time when you start to date is a very trying period for your parents. The better the rapport that you establish with them from the very start, the pleasanter the next few years will be. No one wants to be perpetually bickering over restrictions and dos and don'ts, so try to work out an arrangement which is agreeable to all. You'll have to compromise—*you* more than your parents—but remember that you owe them respect and attention, as they, in turn, owe you trust and appreciation of your intelligence.

The most important thing you can do to prove yourself worthy of that trust is to keep them informed.

Introduce every boy you date to them.
Tell them where you are going.
Tell them when you expect to be home, and make it on time. If you have an agreed-upon curfew, observe it.
If for any reason you'll be late, telephone and let them know.
Don't cheat by going places you know they disapprove of, or sneaking out with people whom you know they don't like.

If you observe these rules, you will win the complete confidence of your mother and father. Why should you want this?

Because you'll be the winner. You'll be allowed, with their blessing, to do almost anything you want within reason, and you'll avoid years of living with restrictions that can hamper or ruin your whole dating life.

## Restrictions on Dating

Your age is the major factor in setting up dating restrictions. Once you are in college, you will be restricted only by the college rules, and the rest is up to your own judgment. If your parents have taught you the right values at home, you will doubtless hold to them all your life, even though you may be subjected to different influences and it may be difficult at times to stick by your ideals. In any case, once you have left home and become independent, it would be ridiculous and unrealistic for your parents to try to impose restrictions on your dating life back home. The only rules they should ask of you are those which involve the comfort of the rest of the family—on use of the car or the family room, keeping the house quiet for sleeping babies, etc.

At the lowest end of the ladder are the thirteen- and fourteen-year-olds who are just starting to date, and who should adhere to reasonably strict laws laid down by their parents.

The restrictions I want to discuss are, therefore, aimed at the middle-teen years—fifteen to seventeen—and if that's where you are, you and your family should adjust hours and limitations accordingly.

As I have talked to young people all over the country, some statistics have emerged. A vast majority of girls, over seventy-five percent, were restricted in some way by their parents. Even boys were expected to stick to certain standards—sixty-one percent, for instance, were supposed to be home by a certain hour. Those who had no restrictions were "expected" to be in at a reasonable hour, and if they weren't their parents lowered the boom. Few of you seemed to be particularly upset about the restrictions, and, in the case of the girls, many were very much in favor of them, because they felt much more secure if there were definite hours to keep and places to stay away from.

Restrictions should never be imposed arbitrarily, or because of lack of trust, although of course the latter often *is* the reason. Restrictions should be set up as a prop for those who need them, as a safeguard to health, as a means of ensuring study time, and to assist young people as they learn to discriminate about when, where, and with whom they date.

In some communities, parents and teen-agers have gotten together and established a dating code. This is an excellent idea. It gives the parents a feeling of confidence in their children's judgment, and the young people a sense of responsibility in making and keeping the rules.

HOW LATE?

Dating hours vary, as I said, with your age and with the customs of the locality in which you live. The hours mentioned here are average for the middle teen, and may be adjusted with your parents' approval.

On weekends, for ordinary dates—movies, gathering at friends' houses, bowling, etc.—twelve to twelve-thirty is a reasonable curfew.

When you go to a dance or prom, add an hour to the announced ending time, to allow for snacks, after-parties, etc.

On weekdays, you should be home by eleven.

Coming-home time for very special occasions—graduation, balls, etc.—must be settled by discussion with your parents.

In all cases, if you are delayed, call your parents *right away*.

HOW OFTEN?

Dates should be restricted to Friday and Saturday nights.

On week nights, you should only go out for school or church functions, or to go someplace with your parents. Exceptions: Gift of theater or concert tickets, weddings, or family celebrations, other *very* special occasions.

WITH WHOM?

Girls who care about their reputations don't go out with "pickups" or people about whom they know nothing. Most young people take the mingling of racial and religious groups as perfectly natural, but parents may have strong objections to their children's going out with members of other races or faiths. This again is something that must be discussed with parents, but until one is independent there is little that can be done except to respect their feelings in this very important matter.

It is wise to stick to your own age group while you're in your middle teens. There is no real objection to a girl's dating a younger boy, but since girls mature faster, boys of her own age or older are more stimulating, and her friends may wonder why she is interested in a younger boy. Older boys are apt to go places and do things that a sixteen- or seventeen-year-old girl is not ready for. Otherwise, any boy who has been introduced to your parents and has met with at least tacit approval (not necessarily enthusiasm) is fair game. After one or two dates, you should know yourself if he's the kind of boy you want to continue to go out with.

WHERE TO?

If your parents say "No!" when you ask if you may go to the Zombie Club, don't go. They may know things about it that you don't, and they're thinking of your safety as well as your reputation. Every town has its dives or unsavory spots. If your date suggests going to one after you've left the house, refuse. You can blame Mom and Dad and say they've forbidden you to go there.

Always tell your family where you're planning to go, and let them know if your plans change. They'll feel relaxed and have all the confidence in the world in you if they know you'll call and say, "Mom, the group is going on to Margie's after the dance. O.K. if I go too?"

## When Girls Ask Boys

Every so often an occasion arises when it's perfectly all right for a girl to ask a boy for a date. A girl may receive an invitation that says, "Bring a date," or often a school or club organizes a girl-ask-boy party. One high school I visited recently—and I'm sure many others have variations of the same idea—has an annual "Twerp Week" or "Dear Season" (I forgot to ask whether they spelled it "Dear" or "Deer") during which each girl tags one boy and asks him to all the festivities planned for that week.

It's also perfectly all right to invite a boy to your house for dinner, but if you don't know him well ask another couple too, or he'll probably think you're making a play for him, and may be scared off.

If your family has given you tickets to the theater, a baseball game, or any special event, don't hesitate to ask a boy to go with you, but pick someone who likes whatever the entertainment is. Don't, for instance, ask the captain of the football team to go to a concert, unless you're sure he's also wild about classical music.

Judging by the number of girls who have questioned me about how to do it, asking a boy for a date sends many of you into a panic, and it shouldn't. The boy will be flattered and pleased that you asked him, and that doesn't harm anybody's stock. How to do it? You ask a boy exactly as he would ask you. You can do it by telephone, this way: "Hi, Jimmy. Mom and Dad just gave me two tickets to the game Saturday, and I was hoping you could go with me. How about it?" Or "Sally's having a 'Bring a Date' party Friday night. Could you go with me?" Then, when he accepts, be sure to give him the necessary details.

TRANSPORTATION

When a girl asks a boy to go somewhere with her, it's up to her to arrange the transportation. If you know he drives and has a car available, you may ask him if he can use his car that night. If you have a car at your disposal, and he has a license but nothing to drive, ask your parents if it's all right for him to drive your car. Either he can arrange his own transportation to your house, or you may pick him up and then let him take over the driving. When you return home, however, the boy should drive you to your house, and then make his own way home. Girls should never be left to drive home alone late at night.

If neither of you drives, you must arrange with your parents, or an older brother or sister, to take you and your date to wherever you're going. You drive to his house and *you* go to the door to get him while the driver waits in the car. And you make arrangements for that driver, or someone else, to pick you up later.

While your date might pay his fare on a bus or subway, and yours too, when you must take more expensive transportation such as a taxi, you should pay. Insist if you must—"No, Hank, this evening is on *me!*" Just as on a regular boy-ask-girl date, Hank must see you to your door; he cannot send you off on one bus while he takes another to his home.

### OTHER EXPENSES

All expenses for the date are the responsibility of the girl when she does the asking. She—or her family—pays for tickets and for any meals involved. She should give him the tickets and any money that will be needed before they start out. Transportation expenses are covered in the preceding paragraph. However, once the occasion for which she asked him—the dance, the show, etc.— is over, he assumes his normal role. For instance, if they decide to go to a snack bar or night club after the theater, the boy should pay for that since it was not a part of the original invitation.

## Ideas for Dates

What'll we do? Where'll we go? I can't help too much because the answer depends on what's available. Nine out of ten of you go to the movies and it's a fine thing to do as long as there are movies around that you haven't seen. In answer to a boy who wrote me and asked, "When you've been going with a girl for a while, what else is there to do besides go to the movies?" Well, I'll list a few suggestions. Some of them won't appeal to you, and others may not be possible because the facilities don't exist in your town. But they may give you an idea or two. Try:

Miniature golf or a driving range.
Bowling.
Roller skating.
Ice skating—at a rink, or better yet on a pond if there's a moon.

Square dancing. Many towns, even in the East, have active groups
which announce their programs in local papers.

Lectures or discussion groups, especially in college towns. Most
people, after the first shock, find them stimulating and interesting.

Church activities. You don't have to be a regular churchgoer to enjoy
many of the activities planned by church youth groups.

Sightseeing tours.

Museums and art galleries.

Television studios—either a tour of a large studio, or watching a show being televised as members of the audience.

Horseback riding.

Fairs, carnivals, or circuses when they're available.

# 21 On Keeping It Cool

## *Why You Want to Keep It Cool*

Let's take up "why" you want to keep it cool first. We all know that things have changed since Grandma was a girl, and a lot of the changes are for the better. Sex has certainly been brought into the open—in fact, the pros and cons are discussed so much that at times the subject threatens to become boring. I am not going to add to that danger by a lengthy discussion of how far you should go; that is really something you have to decide for yourselves according to the moral values you have absorbed from your family and your environment. However, before you decide what you're going to do, you should consider a number of aspects of the problem that are very definitely related to etiquette.

## *The Boy's Role*

Although the final decision on keeping it cool generally rests with the girl, boys certainly must share the responsibility at times. Because I feel their role is sometimes overlooked, I'll start out with some thoughts which every boy should consider before getting too deeply involved with a girl.

You, as well as your dates, have a reputation to worry about. You may think it would be fun to be considered a wolf, and that type does appeal to certain girls; but are they the girls you're really interested in? And you may well defeat your own purpose by getting that sort of a name, for not only will you find there are attractive girls who won't date you, but—if the word circulates—there will also be homes where parents won't make you welcome.

Another serious question is whether or not you really want a girl to capitulate. Whereas you might start out with just the idea of a little "making out"—nothing serious—you may get a more passionate response than you expected, or even wanted. Before your desire gets out of hand, think about whether you want to get deeply involved. Are you serious about that girl, and do you want her to get serious about you?

There is also the matter of fairness—responsibility. If you're not serious, it isn't considered admirable in any league to lead a girl on, with increasingly demanding advances, to thinking you are. Boys have a higher degree of sexual drive and often a higher degree of pleasure in the act of sex itself, which can be very misleading to a girl. Before you let yourself get carried away by your natural impulses, remember that since most girls do not enjoy sex as much unless they feel that their emotions are involved— that they are in love—it will be hard for them to understand that you do not necessarily feel the same way.

## And Now—the Girls

One of the basic purposes of etiquette is to help you improve your relations with other people and make you, personally, more attractive.

Promiscuity—*un*discriminating distribution—is *not* attractive. Nothing given away indiscriminately is valuable. And this is certainly true of sex, perhaps more than of any other thing. To make sex what it should be, to make it worth anything, emotion and meaning must be involved. "Free love" may sound exciting—

a sign of liberated thought, freedom—but think about it from this point of view. Do you want to attract people who simply wish to use you, or do you want sincere admirers? Promiscuity isn't a short cut to authentic popularity; it's only an admission that a person lacks the confidence or ability to gain friends except by desperate measures.

You may say, "Nobody needs to know." But it never, never remains a secret that a girl is generally available. And, of course, any boy who is interested will quickly make it *his* business. If you choose the "free love" route, you may have plenty of dates. Does that mean you're popular? Or attractive? No—it just means that you're available and willing.

There is one sinner with a worse reputation than the girl who is too available; that's the one who goes so far that the boy thinks she *is* available and then she quits. Unfortunately, there are girls who do this deliberately; they want the excitement of some sex but not the danger or complication of giving themselves completely. Others simply get carried away by their emotions, or by a desire to attract or hold a certain boy. Whatever the reason, the tease is the lowest of the low—she's cheating the boys she leads on, and she's cheating herself emotionally; and practically too, because when the word gets around, as it will, her dating life may well be over.

## Responsibilities

Now let's consider the effect of your actions on other people. Many of us would like to be responsible to ourselves only, but in fact this is almost an impossibility. And here is where etiquette comes in again—where your relationship with other people is involved. It is true that most young girls who are promiscuous are not happy, or even satisfied, with their homes and families. But nearly all parents do provide their children with the physical necessities, and most also provide some degree of love or affection. They deserve, therefore, a relative amount of consideration in return. Their reaction to loose behavior on their daughter's part can be selfish—that her actions reflect on *their* morals and the way *they* brought her up. But, more probably, they will be crushed.

They will feel they have failed her and that she is endangering her chances of a good life.

And how about the other members of her family? Even if a younger sister's morals are much stricter, she still may find that her dates expect a willing response to their advances because of her older sister's reputation.

Family pride may prevent a brother from ignoring derogatory remarks about her and her activities, and he may well end up fighting to defend her.

Most serious of all, of course, she could become pregnant. The rate of both illegitimate births and abortions keeps rising. The disastrous effects and potential tragedy for her, the boy, both their families, and the baby are too numerous and too well known for me to go into here. But I do want to make one point: young people are continually lectured on this subject by the adult world —parents, religious leaders, teachers, youth counselors, books, and magazines. After a while, all these warnings, constantly repeated, may seem to become drab clichés—particularly when contrasted with the allure and excitement of love and romance. But simply because warnings are tiresome to hear or read does not mean they aren't valid.

## First Dates

You may have had the misfortune to date an insensitive clod who mauled you and refused to take "No" for an answer simply because he was stronger than you. Happily, he is the exception. Most boys are reasonably sensitive to the atmosphere you create, and respond in kind. After all, they don't like being turned down, so if your attitude says, "Hands off," they won't make much more than an exploratory effort to be sure they've read you right.

It's a cinch to keep it cool if you decide you dislike a boy and don't care whether you ever see him again. Far more often, however, you may not want to kiss on a first date, but you're having fun and very much want the boy to ask you out again. How do you indicate this without having him think you're a stuffed shirt or even that you don't like him? It's fairly simple:

1. You're an interested listener and an enthusiastic talker, but you don't dwell on the subject of sex, dirty jokes, or your friends' love lives.
2. You sit reasonably close to him in the car, but you don't squeeze up tight or put your arm around him.
3. You let him hold your hand in the movies, but you don't keep wiggling around and squeezing his hand.
4. You don't wrap yourself around him like an octopus when you dance.
5. When he takes you to your door, you thank him, chat a moment or two, and go in. If you linger for long, he's practically obligated to kiss you good night.
6. If you really like him and he really wants to kiss you good night, don't make a federal case out of it. Kiss him, but make it a brief, thank-you sort of kiss until you know him better. If you feel strongly that you prefer not to kiss him, don't. Most boys will try for a kiss if the date's been a success, but they don't really expect to get one. All you have to say is "Jim, I had a great time and I want to see you again, but I'd rather wait." This is both honest and flattering, and suggests that you'd like another date. It also makes your kisses worth more when you're ready to give them.

There is protection for your self-esteem in refusing to kiss on a first date. If you've given in and he then never calls again, you'll feel pretty foolish. Wait until you *know* he's interested, and you'll have no cause for regrets. Don't get trapped into thinking you *have* to kiss him to insure his calling again. If he really likes you, don't worry—he'll be around again whether you've kissed him or not!

## As Times Goes On

Inevitably, when you are fond of a boy and continue to go out with him, he is going to want more than a good-night kiss. You may too, unless you prefer him just as a friend. Always bear in mind that each step you take leads to another, and if you don't want your romance to get out of hand you *must* draw a line. It's up to the girl to draw the line, and if she sincerely wants to, and has the strength of her convictions, she'll do it before matters get too difficult. The best way to accomplish this is to avoid situations which automatically provide opportunity and stimulus. Here are a number of ways of improving your chances of keeping it cool, without appearing to be a real square:

Suggest a movie *theater* instead of a drive-in.

Avoid movies that are too sexy.

Don't ask him in after dates unless your parents are still up.

Arrange double dates as often as possible.

Don't wear provocative clothes.

Don't frequent lover's lanes. They're a real hazard; think of any reason to avoid going to one. You're starved—would he take you to a snack bar? You're exhausted—would he mind taking you home early tonight?

Don't go to parties where there will be no chaperone, especially if you know it's likely to turn into a make-out party. If that should happen, get him away on any excuse, or you'll be faced with the old "everyone else is doing it" routine.

Don't let him talk you into a date unless he has definite plans for the evening. Such dates too easily turn into a moonlight drive (dangerous), a midnight swim (more dangerous), or a booze-in-the-glove-compartment party (most dangerous).

If, in spite of all your planning and good intentions, you find you're alone together and his kisses are getting more demanding and his hands are wandering, you can still cool it off. You can get righteous and mad, but if you like the boy this may be the wrong tack. The most diplomatic thing you can do is to introduce some humor into the situation—"Oh Frank, this reminds me of . . ." Giggle about how ridiculous you both must look—anything that will somehow get him to laugh, and you laugh too. Laughter and serious sex just don't mix, and a break of this sort will generally get things back on an even keel.

If you honestly haven't encouraged a boy to make demands, it's perfectly reasonable for you to make him feel a little guilty. "Roy, I've always thought so much of you that I wouldn't have expected you to act like this." This may appeal to his pride enough to slow him up.

If a boy really likes you, wants to continue to see you, and respects you, the simplest, most honest way is best: "Bob, I think we'd better go home. I like you and want to go on seeing you, but I won't feel I can if we get too carried away, so let's move on, O.K.?"

## Blind Dates

I'm afraid there's a universal tendency to expect too much from a blind date; and the only thing that changes this attitude is experience. I have talked to hundreds of girls about blind dates, and nine out of ten regard them as a sort of necessary evil. A blind date is considered better than sitting at home, but the chances are the evening will be a bore. Even if your date is a good friend to a boy you know and like, this is no guarantee that he will be your type, or on a par with the mutual friend.

If you have blind dates often, as many college students do, by the law of averages you'll probably meet one or more boys that you really do have fun with. And that is all you should expect. Accept blind dates if you want to, as long as they are arranged by someone you know, but go into them with the firm idea that they're only for one evening, and enjoy that evening as much as you can. If the date calls back, fine; if not, don't think you're a social flop—he, too, probably just wanted a companion for one night.

### ARRANGING BLIND DATES

Acceptable blind dates are arranged by:

*Older people.* You are visiting Aunt Jane and she asks her friend's son Jack to come for dinner and to take you to a movie or the local hangout.

*A girl you're visiting.* She is asked for a date and tells the boy that she has a guest, so could he arrange with a friend to make it a double date?

*A boy who asks you for a date.* And then inquires if you can get a date for one of his friends.

In these three cases, you actually know the person who is making the arrangements. But dangerous is the date arranged through a chain of people. You are really taking a chance when:

> Your roommate barely knows a boy who telephones and asks her to arrange a date for a friend of his. She hardly knows the caller, and you've never met him, let alone his friend. This is where I say, "Don't go!" Wait until your roommate gets to know the caller better, or until he has introduced her to the potential blind date.

## Going Steady

From an etiquette point of view, there is no objection to going steady. But it does limit your experience in learning how to get along with a number and a variety of people. While you get to know a boy extremely well—possibly as well as your own family—the trouble is that you automatically relax your "company manners" with him, just as you do at home. One could argue that this is a point in favor of going steady—that you can be natural, relaxed, and comfortable with a boy. That's true, but too much togetherness can be tiresome. There's a lot of truth in the old saying "Familiarity breeds contempt." Very often a freer relationship which allows you to see other people and be independent survives far better than the closeness of going steady.

Reactions were mixed in answer to a questionnaire I sent out on the subject of going steady. In general, boys approved of it more than girls, but that might be because they have less difficulty than girls in breaking up and getting back into circulation. A number of girls said they didn't approve of it but went steady anyway—because "everyone does it" and they were afraid they wouldn't have any dates if they didn't. Finally, about 90 percent of those who did approve qualified their answers. Because I'm sure you'll be interested to know what other teen-agers think about the whole subject, I'm listing some of the statements they made:

## FOR GOING STEADY—UNQUALIFIED

Affords security.
A beautiful relationship—enriches life.
You can feel at ease.
Sex problems can be talked out.
You never have to worry about dates.
You get to know a boy better.
A good way to prove feelings for each other.
Everybody my age (sixteen) does.
Usually you can trust the boy more.

## AGAINST GOING STEADY

It ties you down.
It's too serious.
Just a way of being "in."
More fun to play the field.
Plenty of time for that later.
Can be monotonous.
Leads to immorality.
It's unsure and immature.
A "steady" takes advantage of you.
You get too involved.
You get out of circulation.
You can't develop socially and emotionally.

## THOSE WHO SAID YES, IF . . .

You've dated enough to be sure.
You are mature enough.
You're not *too* serious.
It's not *too* binding.
You're sincere—not doing it just to have dates.
Sexual relations don't occur.
You don't mind being tied down.
Neither is too possessive.

## OTHERS SAID "YES, BUT . . ."

It's too restricting—can be a prison.
Can cause heartaches.

It's silly just for security.
Only if the couple is serious enough.
If you want to have fun, don't do it!

There were many other statements, of course, to fit individual cases, but the ones listed were repeated in more or less the same words over and over. In any case, you yourself must decide whether or not going steady is something you want to do, and maybe the best way is to try it once, and then make an intelligent decision. Most adults will probably tell you it's a mistake, but the only way you can be sure is to find out for yourself.

### BREAKING UP

This is very difficult; breaking up is almost never by mutual consent, and someone is usually hurt. It may happen without an explosion, but sometimes it's necessary for the girl or the boy to pick a fight in order to bring things to a head. He may gradually stop calling so often, and then she may hear he's been asking questions about that new girl in his class. What does the girl do? She has two choices. She can call him and ask him to come over and talk it out, and accept the results of that talk. Or she can call on every bit of pride she has and show him she doesn't care by getting back into circulation herself—first. She takes off his ring or any outward sign of the relationship, but she needn't return it immediately; she can wait until she's able to face him without falling apart.

If the shoes's on the other foot and the girl decides it's time to break up, she must stick to her guns. Always make the break face to face. Notes or phone calls are the easy, cheap way to avoid looking someone in the eye. Girls have told me that it has taken them months to end a relationship they're really sick of only because, after a few dateless weekends, they've given in and resumed going steady. It's not easy to sit around waiting for the phone to ring and thinking about what all your friends are doing, but you have to have guts, and if you do there are plenty of ways to help yourself. Here are some ways to spread the word that you're back in circulation:

Ask your best friend to have a "bring-a-date" party, and bring one yourself.

Invite your friends to your house, with an unattached boy for you.

Avoid the places you used to haunt with your steady.

If, as a couple, you were members of a tight group, break away and call some other girls, especially those who are playing the field.

The word spreads quickly, and if you make the effort to be fun and attractive, the phone will soon start ringing again, and you may even find out what you've been missing.

After a breakup, you'll perhaps go through a spell of pure, unadulterated hatred. That's perfectly natural, but do your best not to let it show, and get over it as soon as possible. After all, the guy must be pretty nice if you spent all that time and effort on him, and also he may have friends you'd like to know better. Boys can be mean when they're angry, and they may try to persuade their friends that you're not worth dating. Your attitude can do a lot to prevent this—an air of *It was great fun, but it was just one of those things* is much better than an atmosphere of accusations and recriminations. An ex-steady can be one of the best friends in the world if you both face the fact that the romance is over.

## GOING "STEADILY"

When you have an understanding with a boy that you like him best, that he has *first* call on your attentions, but that you will both go out with other people when you're not together, you're going "steadily." This is a new interpretation of going steady, and in my opinion a sensible one. It avoids all the pitfalls—the too-constant togetherness, the restrictions on your friendships, the overemphasis on being "serious"—and it allows you to meet and know other boys and to stay in circulation. At the same time, you still have the security of an "understanding" and a reasonable assurance of dates with someone you care about.

## STEADY EXPENSES

When a boy and girl are really going steady, his expenses get pretty high. He is probably taking her out on both weekend nights, as well as for snacks after school, and occasionally to other events. Since most boys in their teens have limited funds, steady girl friends should share the expenses some of the time. The boy pays for all tickets for events to which he asks her, and of course he pays when he invites her out for lunch or dinner. But if it's just a stop at a soda fountain, or an afternoon when someone suggests, for instance, that the gang all go to the circus, Sally will help out a great deal if she pays her own way. She can also help by asking the boy to meals at her house, and by getting tickets and inviting him to a show or a game once in a while.

LOVE IN PUBLIC

To have any meaning, love-making must be a private matter between a boy and girl—without the rest of the world as an audience. The subject is so openly discussed and pictured in movies, in books, or on radio and TV today that much of the reticence about making a public spectacle of affection has disappeared. Young people indulge in exhibitions of love-making on the dance floor, in parked cars with other couples present, in fraternity houses, in drive-in movies, in parks, or on beaches. Many of you think that's fine. Others, however, are embarrassed or disgusted, but there's not very much to be done about it except to avoid the particular situation another time.

Simple hand holding on the street, or in the movies, isn't objectionable. But a city street is no place for walking with arms twined around each other. A moving automobile is no place for necking—it's too dangerous. Even hanky-panky in the back seat can distract the driver, and may block his vision in the rear-view mirror.

Real kisses—not just good-night pecks—should be reserved for when you're alone. They should not be a matter of public observation, and people with any natural sense of modesty or self-respect do not wish to invade anyone else's privacy by being thus included in the act.

Sprawling over your date on the beach or in the park, ardent kissing on the dance floor, and making out in movies or theaters are taboo because these things are, believe me, offensive to the people around you. When you're in public, especially with adults around, to make everyone feel comfortable, keep it cool!

# 22 College Weekends

One of the most exciting dates in a girl's life is her first college weekend. The occasion may be a special football game, a winter carnival, or a spring homecoming; whatever the reason, the girls arrive in droves and it's one continuous party for two or three days.

The first time you're invited to a man's college, you'll have a lot of questions about clothes, what activities will go on, etc. Your best source of information is a girl who has been there. If you can't find one, at least talk to friends who have been to other colleges; all house parties have some similarities. Boys do tend to forget important bits of information: for instance, that the Saturday-night dance is formal. Don't be shy about asking your date for the necessary details—it isn't that he didn't mean to tell you; it just didn't occur to him.

A girl pays her own transportation to and from the college. If she is driving, her date should give her the best routes. If she's not coming by car, he should let her know the best way to get there—train schedules, bus connections, or whatever. The boy should meet her when she arrives, or arrange for a friend to be there if, for a very good reason, he cannot make it himself. From that moment on, all expenses are his—food, lodging, everything.

The lodging may be provided by the college—in sorority houses, dormitories, homes of professors. Or the boy may reserve a hotel or motel room for his date, but only if another girl is going to share it with her. Girls should not stay alone in motels or hotels; it is asking for trouble or criticism. If a boy doesn't tell his date beforehand where she will be staying, she must ask, or she's liable to find herself in an awkward position. A young friend of my daughter's arrived for a weekend and discovered she was expected to sleep on the couch in her date's living room. She was afraid to walk out with no place to go, so she couldn't leave until the following morning. She was simply forced to make the best of a difficult situation. Not only did she have to convince her date that he couldn't join her on the couch, but she was made miserable by the thought of her family's and friends' reactions to her evening's lodgings. All of this could have been so easily avoided had she thought to ask, "Where will I be staying?"

To protect yourself from embarrassing situations, to make the weekend run smoothly, and to win yourself another invitation, set standards for yourself based on the following *dos* and *don'ts*. They will help you to have a good time, and you'll help make the weekend a success for your date and everyone else you meet, in any college, any place, any time.

*Don't* forget accessories as you pack. "Blue dress—what goes with it? Belt, jewelry, pocketbook, etc."

*Do* keep your luggage neat and *compact*. If you can drive your car right to the door of your accommodations, you're in luck and can splurge, but if you're arriving by train or bus, and your date has to carry a big suitcase and three or four bundles through the depot and down the street, the weekend will not be off to an auspicious start.

*Do* greet the chaperone or housemother at the sorority house or dormitory in a friendly, enthusiastic way.

*Don't* ignore the other girls staying with you; not only may they be fun to know, but you may need a female friend before the weekend is over.

*Don't* take up more than your share of closet or drawer space, monopolize the bathroom, or leave your clothes and cosmetics all over the room.

*Do* be sure to pack *everything* when the weekend is over, and leave the room as neat as you found it.

*Do* say good-bye to the chaperones and thank them with sincerity.

*Don't* wait for introductions at fraternity—or other—parties. You may be thought a snob when actually you're only shy. Strike up a conversation with anyone who appeals to you, and he'll just think you friendly, not pushy.

*Do* dance with anyone who cuts in, unless he's tight or offensive.

*Do* whatever your date has planned—cheerfully—even if you'd rather be somewhere else.

*Don't* be jealous if your date looks at another girl, and *don't* show your disappointment if he's not all you thought he'd be.

*Don't* try to be the house-party queen; *do* devote your attention and enthusiasm to your own date. *Do* show appreciation, and *do* have a good time!

Follow these simple suggestions, and I know you will.

# TRAVEL TALK

# 23 Planning Your Trip

There's no doubt about it, planning a trip—whether it be a drive across the United States, a weekend in Bermuda, a few days of skiing in Canada, or six weeks in Europe—can be almost as much fun as the trip itself. But added to the joy of poring over maps, collecting addresses and suggestions from friends, and planning your wardrobe are certain practical preparations. Dream of those medieval castles all you want, but you may have awfully sore feet after actually touring one if you forget to pack comfortable shoes. Also, the knowledge that you'll have a good night's sleep in a decent bed will make the day's sightseeing much more pleasant.

## Students' Cards and Passports

If you're going abroad, be sure to obtain, through your school or college, a "student card." These cards will open doors for you all over Europe and will guarantee you substantial reductions in the prices of travel, tickets to many spectacles, entrance fees to museums and educational institutions, and, in some cases, your accommodations. Although not accepted officially, they also serve as identification should you find yourself without your passport.

It ordinarily takes one week to ten days to obtain a passport. Before peak tourist seasons, it may take more, so plan ahead. You must appear in person to present your filled-out form, and you must have the required photographs. You should plan to keep your passport with you *at all times*. With it—should you get into trouble —you can prove your nationality and call on your consulate immediately; without it you are open to suspicion and the possibility of being held until you can prove your citizenship or the legality of your presence.

## *Reservations*

Most of you who plan a driving trip, either in the States or abroad, won't worry about advance reservations for much of the time. And most of the way it will work out beautifully; there are youth hostels, off-the-beaten-track inns and pensions, or plain motels almost everywhere. In Europe, many of the small inns or pensions will call ahead to your next destination and reserve a room for you. They have reciprocal agreements with other inns, and are glad to do it. During the summer vacation, many foreign universities open their dormitories to traveling students. These accommodations are often more comfortable than the crowded youth hostels, and have fewer rules and restrictions. Your student card is your ticket of admission. In the tourist cities and resorts, however, every bed is apt to be filled during peak vacation seasons. While it sounds very romantic and independent to say, "We'll just go when and where the spirit moves us," it can be mighty discouraging to find, on a night when a downpour prevents sleeping in a hayfield, that every bed in the nearby town is filled. In short, when you are heading for a spot which is a mecca for tourists, get a reservation in advance. Pamplona during the running of the bulls, Salzburg during the music festival, all cities during fair or festival seasons are filled to overflowing, and, without reservations, you just can't count on finding a place to unpack your suitcase.

Girls traveling in the United States during the summer should take advantage of the call-ahead reservation service. Most good motels are affiliated with, if not actually members of, a chain or group of some sort. They will reserve space at your next stop until a certain hour. If you are not sure of your arrival time, you may pay in advance at the motel where you are, guaranteeing a room for you at the next place regardless of what time you arrive. If you don't know how far you'll be by dark and must leave lodgings to chance, try to stop by 5 P.M. Shortly after that hour every room along the main roads may well be filled.

# *Travel Agencies*

The easiest way to make reservations is through a travel agent. They can make suggestions that will fit your budget, and it costs no more than doing it yourself, except for an occasional small charge for certain hotel reservations. They also provide information on airplanes, buses, trains, or boats, and will make those reservations for you, if you wish. A good agency will do as little or as much as you want—from simply making a reservation to and from your destination, to planning and organizing every day of your trip. If you are anticipating a summer trip abroad, be sure to make reservations for your return, even though you may be uncertain about the exact date. You can no doubt estimate pretty closely, and if you have the reservation you're safe. You can always cancel it if plans change, but if you wait until the middle of your trip to plan your return you'll find it almost impossible to get home when you want to.

Another way in which a travel agency can help you is to tell you what documents you will need for each country you plan to visit. They will tell you just how to go about getting passports, visas, and health certificates. They will take care of many of the details which need not be done by you in person.

Most oil companies have their own agencies which map the best driving routes anywhere in the world. Some of them also provide excellent guidebooks, and, for girls traveling together, a reliable guidebook is essential. It's very difficult, in unfamiliar surroundings, to judge a place by its outside appearance, and a recommendation in an accepted guidebook can keep you out of all sorts of embarrassing or unpleasant situations.


# *Funds for Travelers*

Whether you're planning to travel on $5 a day or $25, you must not carry too much cash. But, at the same time, you should have adequate funds easily available, especially in case of an emergency such as an accident, illness, or theft. The answer lies in traveler's checks. These are bought at any bank by simply paying for them in

cash—the amount you wish in checks, plus a very small fee for the service. You sign them once at the bank when you buy them, and you sign again when you wish to cash one or use it to make a purchase. Because they are already paid for, they are accepted as cash anywhere in the world, and yet, because the two signatures must match, they are not much use, if stolen, to anyone but an expert forger. Furthermore, if they are lost or stolen, you simply notify the place where you purchased them—immediately. Payment is stopped, and no one else may use them. When you buy the checks, you are given a slip on which to fill in the check numbers and amounts and you should keep this slip separate from the checks and in the safest place you can think of, because you must report these numbers in case of loss.

## Your Itinerary

I'm all for traveling as foot-loose and fancy-free as possible, but, once your plans begin to take form, you must have some sort of written itinerary—and you must stick to it. Whether your check-points are every other day, or once in every ten days, is something to be decided between you and those at home. But emergencies

can arise in the family which may require that you be reached immediately. If your family knows where you have been and where you will be within a day or two, the Red Cross, the state police, or an American consulate abroad can usually locate you in a matter of hours. If you don't know when you leave home exactly where you will be staying, make plans to check in for messages and mail at an American Express office, a branch of your father's bank or business. or, wherever possible, with family friends.

## Luggage

The most important requirements for luggage are that it be compact and light. *Compact* because of limited space in airplanes, in cabins on a ship, in foreign cars, or on the back of a motor scooter, and *light* because most of the time you'll have to carry it yourself. Boys may prefer duffel bags to suitcases, for they are more portable and easier to stow away. But, if a girl wants to have a dress looking fresh for a special occasion, she had better stick to a suitcase.

Every piece of luggage should carry a tag with your name and address clearly printed on it. Many a traveler has had a lost suitcase returned because he took this precaution. For easy identification of his suitcases, the smart traveler puts a strip of colored masking tape on each bag. It really speeds things up if you can tell a porter, 'My bags are the ones with the two red stripes."

Try to pack your bags so that the things you will need immediately are on top. If you take a little time in planning and doing your packing, the bottom layers may often be left neatly folded and unmussed for days or even weeks. If you don't already have too many pieces of luggage, a small overnight bag with nightclothes, cosmetics, toothbrush, etc., helps you avoid a great deal of lugging of heavy bags. When you travel by car, you can simply lock the big bags in the trunk and take only the little one into the motel or inn.

Your bags will get increasingly messy after a number of one-night stands, and every so often you should take everything out and repack, if you wish your clothes to remain neat. Before crossing a border or returing home, remember that it will be quicker and that you will feel much more comfortable, when the customs inspector opens your bags, if the clothes are neatly folded and your most intimate possessions are not staring at him from the top of the suitcase.

## Your Wardrobe

It's just plain common sense to take as much drip-dry clothing as possible on any trip. Getting laundry done is a big problem when you're constantly on the move, and for a boy two or three pairs of trousers that will dry on the towel rack overnight, and a couple of drip-dry shirts that can be worn right into the shower, washed, and hung on a hanger to dry, are almost all that will be needed. T-shirts and turtlenecks that need no ironing, a sweater or two, a sports jacket, and a raincoat plus the usual accessories—socks, drip-dry underwear, one or two ties, bathing suit, etc.—complete the lucky male's wardrobe. A suit should be added if he expects to be invited to diplomatic parties or to somewhat formal homes, to attend church services, or to dine in fine restaurants.

Girls have far more planning to do. I won't attempt to suggest wardrobes for each country or season, but I will make a few suggestions which should help you plan your clothing for any place, any time.

If you choose clothes in one color range, you can keep accessories to a minimum. Shoes and pocketbooks are heavy and bulky, so if one pair of heels will go with all your good clothes you'll save on both space and weight.

Be sure that your sightseeing shoes are the most comfortable you can find; nothing can turn a trip into a fiasco more quickly than sore, blistered feet.

I mentioned drip-dries above, but I repeat this most especially for the girls—underwear, blouses, and summer dresses can and should be bought in quick-drying, wrinkleproof fabrics. Don't ever hang anything on a metal hanger to dry without first covering the metal with toilet paper or tissues. Rust stains don't come out easily!

Orlon sweaters wash and dry better than wool.

Don't forget a bathrobe. Many pensions and small hotels do not have private bathrooms and you'll need that robe to get to the W.C. down the hall. You'll also be more comfortable in a robe if a waiter brings you breakfast in bed at a luxury resort or hotel.

No matter what sort of trip you're planning, take one dressy outfit, even if it means an extra pair of shoes. You just never know when the chance of a lifetime will strike, and it would be a shame to miss it because you had "nothing to wear."

A suit is a must because it's so versatile. Take the jacket off when it's warm, put it on when it's cool, and you'll be comfortable in any climate. A variety of blouses to go with the skirt gives the illusion of a number of different outfits, but takes little space.

Dresses with sweaters or jackets are ideal for travelers; like suits, they are adaptable, and the costume changes if you simply remove the jacket.

For your travel coat, choose one which is water repellent so that you won't also need a raincoat.

Shorts and slacks are fine for traveling by car in the United States as long as you're not planning to arrive at an elegant hotel or restaurant in them. They're also all right for national parks and resort areas, but if you're planning on serious sightseeing—in Williamsburg, Virginia; Washington, D.C.; or any of our bigger cities—be sure you have a skirt handy to slip into before you arrive.

Most European women do not wear shorts or slacks on the city streets, though they do wear them at resorts. This is especially true in the Latin countries. Therefore, you will be a much better representative of America if you follow their example. Be as chic as you want—short skirt and all—but stay away from the pants unless you're taking part in some sport, or are at the beach, the mountains, or a country home. This is even truer in some small towns. Rural people may be truly offended by the sight of a girl in short shorts or too-tight slacks; even if they're not offended, they may embarrass you to death with their whispers and giggles.

Take at least one fairly full-skirted dress for plane or train travel. Short, tight skirts may look great on you but to stay modest in them while trying to get comfortable for a snooze on the plane is well-nigh impossible.

Choose a pocketbook that is large enough to hold everything including a hairbrush and your passport and other papers. A shoulder-strap bag is ideal and leaves your hands free for things like picture taking or carrying luggage.

Keep a scarf in your purse. While it isn't always required that you wear a head covering in a church or cathedral, it is often the custom. And furthermore it's a handy thing to have on a windy day.

Don't feel you have to take a lifetime supply of cosmetics, toothpaste, and such with you. There *are* stores all over the world, and although you may not always find your favorite brand of lipstick, you *will* find an acceptable substitute.

Do carry soap and disposable washcloths if you're going abroad. Many hotels do not provide them.

Try to leave with a half-empty suitcase. Wherever your travels may take you, there will be new and exciting things you'll want to bring home with you, and if you plan well you won't have to add the cost and the burden of an extra suitcase to carry them.

# 24 From Here to There

## *Motels*

The chances are, if you're driving, you'll spend many more nights in motels than hotels. I have already discussed using their reservation services on a day-to-day basis: if you think there may be difficulty about getting into a certain motel in a certain area, you should write ahead for a firm reservation. A letter for any sort of motel—or hotel—reservation, should include all the information contained in the following sample:

Road's End Motel
Silver Lakes
Montana

Dear Sirs:
    Please reserve one double room (twin beds preferred), with bath for the night of July 5, 1968. We expect to arrive at about 6 p.m.
    Please confirm as soon as possible. Thank you for your trouble.

                                    Sincerely,

165 Oak Street
Hagerstown, Maryland 25961

I love roadside motels. You don't face the problem of appearing disheveled and weary in a crowded lobby, and there's no bevy of doormen or bellboys to be tipped. You can get your own ice and sodas from handy machines, and, in summer, most motels offer the opportunity of a refreshing swim in a pool.

    There are no rules for overnight guests beyond the ordinary ones of consideration for your neighbors: keep the TV or radio low, don't slam doors, and speak quietly at night in the corridors.

    In motels, as well as hotels, the towels, ash trays, and ice buckets are meant to remain there. It costs millions of dollars each year to replace the articles people take away as "souvenirs." Don't do it!

Make yourself neat and presentable when you go to the dining room, just as you would at any good restaurant. If there is none connected with the motel, the manager, or clerk, will be glad to recommend one nearby.

Try not to depart with the room key in your pocket. As you leave the motel for the last time, place the key on the bureau and let the door remain open. If, by mistake, you do take the key, return it by mail as quickly as possible.

For a one-night stay, you need leave no tip; for longer, you should leave fifty cents a night for the maid. Put it on a desk or table, in an envelope marked "Chambermaid."

At very large and elaborate motels, or those located in a city, your car is not generally parked by your room, and there are bell-boys to carry your luggage. They are tipped the same as a hotel bellboy—twenty-five cents minimum for each bag they carry.

## Hotels

When you wish to stay right in a city, or if you're traveling abroad, you are more likely to stay in a hotel. Make your reservations ahead of time and be sure also to have a written confirmation. If you're late in making a reservation, send a telegram or telephone, but *never* arrive in a big city anywhere without knowing that you have a place to stay.

Let's follow Joan and Pam during an overnight stay in Mid-City at the Central Hotel, which is typical of *all* hotels.

On a rainy afternoon they arrive by taxi from the airport, and the doorman takes their bags, helps them out of the car, and holds an umbrella over them while they pay the fare and go from street to entrance. Had they simply gotten out of a cab (with no luggage) and gone in, he would not have been tipped, but for the extra service, in the rain, Joan gives him a quarter.

They register at the desk (using "Miss" before their names), and show, if asked, the confirmation of their reservation. Then a bell-boy gets the room key, picks up their bags, leads the way to the elevator, and finally to their room. There, he opens the blinds, checks the heat or air-conditioning, turns on the bathroom light, and opens the closet. Pam tips him twenty-five cents for each bag he has carried, and if there are only one or two, an extra quarter for opening up the room.

They are hot and thirsty, so Joan calls Room Service and asks for Cokes. She signs the bill when the waiter arrives with them, and gives him a twenty-five-cent tip.

The girls have friends in town and, after a short rest, they call them. They agree to meet in the lounge of the hotel, rather than having a noisy group in their room. When the others leave, Pam and Joan, still tired, decide to have dinner at the hotel. After their meal, they leave the waiter a tip of a minimum of fifteen percent, possibly twenty percent if the service has been extra special.

Back in their room are the clothes they had given the valet earlier to be pressed. They do not need to leave him a tip; the service will be charged on their hotel bill.

After a good night's sleep, Pam and Joan decide it would be fun to have breakfast sent to their room. They comb their hair, put on bathrobes, and wait in bed, if they wish. The waiter sets up the breakfast table wherever they ask him to, and he is tipped before he leaves the room—approximately fifteen percent of the bill, but no less than fifty cents. Joan and Pam decide that it's awfully expensive to order meals in your room—in addition to the tip you must give the waiter, the hotel adds a room service charge.

After they are dressed and packed, they call the front desk for a bellboy to take the bags down. Again they must tip him twenty-five cents per bag. They also leave one dollar in an envelope marked for the chambermaid.

They check out at the desk, leaving a forwarding address if they want to, and then pay their bill at the cashier's window. The doorman hails a cab from the stand, but the bellboy loads the car, so the doorman is not tipped again for this minimum service.

Although Pam and Joan enjoyed the comforts and services of the hotel, I think, if they're traveling alone, they'll look for simpler accommodations at their next stop!

European hotels are much the same as ours, but there is one difference. All services, except accommodations, are handled by a *concièrge* and he may present you with a separate bill, which generally includes a fifteen or twenty percent tip. You then just add a small amount—possibly the change from the bill.

## Planes

Travel by plane is so common these days that little instruction is necessary, but there is a first time for everyone, and there are a few things you should know.

The *only* people who are tipped when you travel by air (other than waiters in airport restaurants and attendants in checkrooms or rest rooms) are the porters who carry your luggage from the entrance of the airport to the check-in counter, and from the baggage claim counter to your transportation from the airport after your flight.

Once your bags are checked in and weighed, you won't see them again until they are unloaded at your destination. Only the smallest pieces can be carried onto the plane with you, because nothing hard or solid is allowed on the overhead racks. So take only those things that will fit *under* your seat.

If there is a delay in your departure time, get a book or magazine and sit down patiently in view of the board showing the flight schedule. Don't keep pestering the men at the counters for information; it will be posted as soon as it's available. Keep your eye on the board for gate numbers, too; sometimes it's difficult to understand the loud-speaker announcements.

The man at the check-in counter gives you a slip with your seat number if seats are reserved. Show it to the stewardess when you board, and she will help you find your seat.

Wear loose, comfortable clothes, wrinkle-resistant if possible.

Carry a small extra bag or case with things to make your trip comfortable:

1. A pair of scuffs, or socks, so that you can take your shoes off. Bare or stocking feet can get quite cold in an airplane.
2. An orlon sweater or a stole if you're traveling in summer clothes, for the same reason.
3. Disposable washcloth.
4. Miniature toothbrush and toothpaste—awfully refreshing to use after a nap.

5. A book, a puzzle book, knitting, or any favorite time passer.

Don't take more than your own pillow or blanket from the rack above you. If you wish extras, ask the stewardess for them.

Check behind you before you let your seat fly back. If the person in back of you is holding a cup of coffee, or leaning forward, the results can be disastrous.

Talk to the person next to you if he, or she, is responsive, but don't force the conversation if you detect no spark of interest.

If you get off at intermediate stops, listen for your departure announcement. Don't assume that the plane will wait until you finish your coffee.

Don't dawdle in the washrooms; there are always other passengers waiting.

Obey "No Smoking" and "Fasten Seat Belt" signs promptly. Aside from the safety factor, it makes the stewardess's job easier.

## Trains

An overnight train trip used to be one of the greatest thrills in my life. I still think of it as tremendous fun, and if you know what to do and how to do it, you'll enjoy it too.

Unless a higher fixed rate is posted, porters in a railroad station are tipped twenty-five cents a bag—more for extra-large ones. In foreign countries you tip their equivalent of a quarter.

Space is the greatest problem in most Pullman accommodations —a berth or a roomette has practically none. Even a "bedroom" can only hold a minimum amount of luggage. So pack a small overnight bag to keep with you and let the porter stow your big bags at the end of the car.

People at the same table in a dining car usually chat casually, but it's unwise to go into your life history or exchange confidences. Keep it impersonal.

You are seated by a headwaiter, you order by writing your choices on a pad, and you tip exactly as in any other restaurant— fifteen percent is the minimum, and *never* less than twenty-five cents.

In a Pullman section, when you are seated facing forward, it is polite to ask the other occupant of your section if he objects to riding backward, especially if he is an older person. If it does bother him, offer him a seat beside you, or take the backward one yourself—provided, of course, that you're not inclined toward motion sickness.

Occupants of berths must stop talking as soon as other passengers go to bed. If you are with friends and wish to stay up later, go to the club car. But tell the porter to make up your berth so he can finish his work. Passengers in accommodations with doors may talk quietly, but partitions are thin and, if you're likely to giggle or forget where you are, it's better to go quietly to bed.

You have to be almost double-jointed to dress and undress in a berth or roomette, but it can be done. Just wear something that is not difficult to get in and out of. In a Pullman you wash up for the night and get as ready for bed as you can in the ladies' or men's room, then into the berth and through the contortions of getting into your nightclothes. The clothes you remove go into the little hammock strung by the wall for this purpose.

Stewards in the club car are tipped fifteen percent of your check; if you order something in your Pullman, the porter who brings it receives a minimum tip of a quarter.

The Pullman porter usually gets a dollar a night from each passenger.

## Ships

A ship—especially a "student ship," loaded with boys and girls from schools and colleges—is something like a club. Everyone is a member and makes friends as fast as possible with anyone who looks congenial.

There are few rules to worry about on these special ships; dress is informal and the only commitment you have is to be prompt for meals at the fixed times. You make your table reservation in the dining room immediately before, or after, the ship sails. Breakfast, after a night of dancing and partying, is often skipped entirely—unless you can persuade a kindly steward to bring a snack to your cabin. For lunch and dinner you must sit at your assigned table, and your waiter is tipped at the end of the voyage. Each passenger gives him a minimum of a dollar for each day.

You will undoubtedly be sharing your cabin with several other people, so any luggage that you don't need during the voyage should be sent to the hold. You can plan your packing so that one bag will contain everything you need for those few days. And do keep all your belongings in your own section of the cabin.

The cabin steward also gets at least one dollar from each occupant for each day. If he has brought you food or drinks, taken care of you if you've been seasick, or performed any other special services, he should receive more.

The deck steward, if you have taken a deck chair, should get two dollars, the bath steward, one; and the headwaiter, two dollars.

A word of warning about shipboard romances. Do all the dating, dining, dancing, and romancing you want with your new-found Romeo, but hold back a little. It's just possible that you may never hear from him again after you leave the ship. If you do, so much the better, but you can save yourself a lot of heartache and disillusionment if you tell yourself from time to time, "I don't *really* know him, or whether he's left anyone behind him." Just keep it cool; don't fall hook, line, and sinker till the letters start to arrive after you're back on land.

# 25 Your American Image

## *The First Impression—Your Appearance*

Whether you are traveling from here to Kalamazoo or Timbuktu, you represent the place you come from. And when you're on the move—not staying in one place long enough to become known—

the only way people can judge you, or the place you come from, is by your appearance.

If you *look* grubby—dirty, unshaven, motheaten, uncombed—that's exactly what strangers will think you *are*. Sure, you and your group realize you're the salt of the earth, but the man sitting across from you on the plane, or the waiter serving you a coffee at a sidewalk café, has no way of knowing this. So spruce up a little when you travel—especially in a foreign country, where it's terribly important to make the best impression you can. Furthermore, it shows appreciation and respect for the place and the people you're visiting.

I'm *not* recommending that girls get all dressed up to hop on a motor scooter or a bus. Decent-looking slacks or Levi's on the scooter or in a car, and a skirt and sweater or everyday cotton dress, with flats, on a bus are fine, as long as they are clean and neat. A trip on a plane or train requires a little more effort. Although clothes, as I said in the last chapter, should be comfortable, airplane passengers *do* dress up a bit.

The same goes for the traveling male. When you're on a plane, or a first-class train, leave the faded jeans in your duffel bag. A clean pair of slacks, a shirt and tie, a sports jacket, socks, and a pair of shoes that stay on are the right clothes.

We asked hundreds of teen-agers what clothes they usually traveled in, and whether they would like some advice on this. Some of you, especially the boys, replied that you don't want to bother to dress up when you're on the move, but many more were interested in knowing what's right. So, while I know there'll be a lot of moans and groans when I say no jeans and dirty sweatshirts, I must say it, because a little care about the way you look will get you a lot more respect and admiration from the people you meet than an appearance that can only suggest laziness, ignorance, or a "just don't care" attitude.

## Next—Your Attitude

The major part of this chapter is concerned with traveling abroad. In this country, you'll make the same impression in California as you will in Virginia, provided you look and act the same way, but your effect on the natives of Italy may be startlingly different! What may be perfectly normal behavior here can seem very far out elsewhere.

The main thing to remember is that you're a guest. As such, you must take care not to offend the citizens of the country you're visiting. You may not always know what will annoy them, so I'll try to give you a little help. Read the following suggestions; then sprinkle your attitude with a liberal dose of thoughtfulness, of interest in what you're seeing, of enthusiasm for new sights and experiences, and with an effort to fit into strange ways, and you are bound to get more enjoyment out of your trip.

Foreigners are more effusive than we are in their thanks and in showing admiration. If you want them to believe in your appreciation, don't hold back—*gush* a little.

People abroad love flowers and they send them on all sorts of occasions. If you really want to make a hit, send a bouquet to last night's hostess or to the girl you hope to date.

Don't compare everything to the United States. We may have taller buildings, bigger cars, and better hamburgers, but not everyone in the world thinks these things are the be-all and end-all, and natives of each country have pride in their accomplishments and natural wonders. Believe me, every nation has plenty of both.

Be adaptable. If everything is closed from one to four and your shopping and sightseeing are interrupted, don't fume and growl. Roll with the punch; take a siesta yourself and you'll enjoy the rest of the day much more. You may think the meal hours are crazy, but remember the old cliché—when in Rome, do as the Romans do!

Don't assume that everything should be a bargain. Years ago it was the custom to try to get people in marketplaces and shops to lower prices—it was really a game. It still may be in some rural areas, but in cities and on well-traveled routes a price tag means exactly what it says.

Don't be pushy. Europeans are much more patient than we are and often more polite; they look with horror—as they should—at "line crashers."

Speaking of politeness, older people are treated with great consideration and respect in foreign countries, so go out of your way to be on your best behavior in their presence.

Don't *stare!* What may seem picturesque or odd to you—a Greek gentleman toying with his "worry beads," for instance—is perfectly natural to him and he'll be justifiably insulted if you gawk at him.

Americans have the reputation of being terribly loud. You young people can help to dispel that impression if you bend over backward to speak softly and keep your squeals and giggles to a minimum.

Bone up on any country you plan to visit. If you possibly can, learn a few phrases in its language, such as "please," "thank you," "you're welcome," "how much is it?" "where is?" "yes," and "no." Then don't hesitate to use these phrases, and as much of the language as you know, no matter how haltingly or poorly pronounced. The natives will not laugh at you, I promise; they are pleased and flattered when we even *try* to speak their language. Also, learning a little of the local history will not only impress the friends you make, it will add tremendously to the pleasure of your sightseeing.

When you wish to take a picture of someone, ask his permission. He'll probably love it, but if you surprise him by snapping the photo before he knows it he'll feel like something out of *The Old Curiosity Shop*. The very nicest thing you can do is to get names and addresses and send back prints when your film is developed.

Boys—take it easy in approaching the native girls, especially in Latin countries. European women are fast becoming emancipated, but many are still much more old-fashioned than they look, and you have to go through proper channels to arrange an introduction. Rushing in without one can defeat you before you even start.

Table manners are somewhat different abroad, but don't worry about that. If your American manners are good they will be recognized, but never criticized.

Try the food specialties of each country. You'll miss a lot if you stick to American-type food and restaurants all the time, even though they are found almost everywhere.

Don't forget thank-you notes. Just because you may never see a person again is no reason not to show your appreciation. The least you can do when someone has given you a bed, or a meal, or helped you out in any way, is to write a note promptly. Foreigners are meticulous about this sort of thing, so let's prove that we know what to do, too!

## *For Girls Only*

There is safety in numbers. If you're traveling with a friend, or two or three, you are pretty safe in joining a congenial group of boys— as long as you girls stick together. Teen-agers from the same country tend somehow to find each other, and under the casual sort of traveling conditions they move about in there is certainly nothing wrong so far as morals and etiquette are concerned with self-introductions and just plain getting together.

When you're alone, it's a different story. Wolves in sheep's clothing are still around, and it isn't always possible, even for a much older and more experienced woman, to make an accurate judgment of a man she's talked to for only a short time. This includes older men; young girls are apt to assume that their interest is purely fatherly and friendly, and this is not necessarily so.

I have no objection to striking up a conversation with a stranger on a plane, in a dining car, on a bus, or in a hotel dining room. Not only is it boring to have no one to talk to, but it is very unfriendly not to respond amicably to a casual attempt at conversation—as long as you keep it casual! If you really feel that this is a man you want to see again, give him the address of the next point in your trip *where you will be staying with, or traveling with, other people.* If your paths won't cross during your travels, ask him if it's possible for him to see you back at home. That way, you can get to know him in familiar surroundings. Here are the rules, and if you want to avoid sticky or even dangerous situations, take them to heart.

*Don't* give the address or phone number of your destination, unless you are staying with friends and plan to see the man in their company.

*Don't* accept an invitation to any meal or entertainment en route.

*Don't* make a date for the future unless you can be sure it will be a double—or group—date.

*Don't* accept any sort of gift; it automatically puts you under obligation.

*Don't* get personal. Keep your life history, inner feelings, and ambitions to yourself, and don't pry into his.

*Don't* hitchhike—or pick up hitchhikers. You are setting the stage for possible serious trouble if you allow yourself to be shut up in a car with a total stranger.

To sum up, the rules are simple. Always put your best foot forward. Be natural, be considerate, be inquiring, and be enthusiastic. Traveling is the most broadening experience in the world, and to me it's the greatest fun too.

# TIPPING AT
# A GLANCE

I was talking to a high school group recently and the subject of tipping came up. Surprisingly, some of the students never tipped; they didn't think it was necessary at their age. I asked if they were aware that waitresses, cab drivers, hairdressers, and others who perform services rely heavily on tips and that in many jobs the major part of an individual's income is derived from tips.

This fact simply had not occurred to these young people and no one had bothered to point it out. Please, look at tipping from the other fellow's side. Should a waiter be penalized because he has been assigned to wait on you? Is it fair to expect the same service that an adult would if you are not prepared to pay at the same rate?

Admittedly, the practice of tipping occasionally gets out of hand, and there are times when you can rightfully refuse to tip at all—when the service is really bad. But, if it has been good, teen-agers, like everyone else, must accept the responsibility of paying for it.

Tipping varies according to geographical area—city and country—and according to the luxury of the surroundings. When an exact amount is not prescribed—where the guideline might say "fifteen or twenty percent"—teen-agers may certainly pay the lesser amount. Otherwise, they should follow the example of the adults.

The following chart lists the most frequently faced tipping situations and shows the correct amount to be given.

| WHO? | WHEN? | HOW MUCH? |
|---|---|---|
| **RESTAURANTS** | | |
| Waiters, waitresses | In ordinary restaurants | 15% of bill |
| | In luxury restaurants, hotels, night clubs | 20% of bill |
| Headwaiter | When he simply shows you to your table | No tip |

| WHO? | WHEN? | HOW MUCH? |
|---|---|---|
|  | If he rearranges tables to accommodate your group or performs other special services | $1 or $2 |
| Checkroom attendant | When you check anything—coat, hat, parcel, etc. | 25 cents |
| Ladies' room attendant | If no service is rendered | No tip |
|  | If towel is offered and used, or other service given | 25 cents |
| Soda fountain | If limited to snacks—ice cream, coffee, etc. | No tip |
| Lunch counter | When any food is served | 15% of bill—never less than 10 cents |
|  | When order is just coffee, Coke, etc. | No tip |
| Curb service or drive-in | For snacks only | No tip |
|  | When meal is ordered | 15% of bill. Some curb-service restaurants, however, do not permit tipping. |

## HOTELS

| WHO? | WHEN? | HOW MUCH? |
|---|---|---|
| Dining-room waiter | When in a transient hotel, each meal | 15% of bill—never less than 25 cents |
|  | For stay at a resort—same waiter every meal | Approximately 10% of total hotel bill—tip at last meal |
|  | When your waiter or table is changed each meal | Tip the usual 15% |
| Headwaiter | When he just leads you to table | No tip |
|  | On extended stay | $2 or $3 per week |
| Room waiter | When breakfast or other meal is served in room | 15% of bill, never less than 50 cents, in addition to service charge made by hotel |

| WHO? | WHEN? | HOW MUCH? |
|---|---|---|
| Chambermaid | When you stay for one night | 50 cents per person |
| | For extended stay | $2 per week per person |
| Doorman | When he opens taxi or hotel door | No tip |
| | When he carries luggage | 25 cents for one or two bags |
| | When he gets you a taxi other than from stand in front of hotel | 25 cents |
| Bellboys | When they page you | 25 cents |
| | When they bring beverages, packages, telegrams, etc., to your room | 25 cents |
| | When they carry luggage | 25 cents a bag |
| | For opening up room— turning on lights, air conditioner, etc. | 25 cents in addition to luggage-carrying charge |
| Porter | For delivering or picking up a trunk | 50 cents |
| Shoeshine boy | Whenever service is used | 25 cents |

## MOTELS

| | | |
|---|---|---|
| Maids | For one-night stay | No tip |
| | For extended stay | 50 cents a night for one room |
| Bellhops | In luxury motels, when they lead you to, and open up, your room | 25 cents |
| | When they carry luggage | 25 cents a bag |
| Others | Same as hotels | |

## PLANES AND AIRPORTS

| | | |
|---|---|---|
| Steward, stewardess | On all airplanes | No tip |

| WHO? | WHEN? | HOW MUCH? |
|---|---|---|
| Airport porters | When they carry luggage between airport door and check-in or baggage claim counter | 25 cents a bag |
| Attendants at ticket counters | | No tip |

## TRAINS AND RAILROAD STATIONS

| | | |
|---|---|---|
| Porters | When they carry luggage to or from trains | 25 cents a bag or more if rate is posted. Sometimes 35 cents |
| Dining-car waiters | At any meal served in dining car | 15% of bill—no less than 25 cents |
| Bar-car steward | For any drinks served in bar car | 15% of bill—no less than 15 cents |
| | Drinks brought to Pullman car | 25 cents |
| Pullman porter | For each night, per person | 50 cents to $1 |

## TAXI DRIVERS

| | | |
|---|---|---|
| | When fare is under 50 cents | 15 cents |
| | When fare is between 50 cents and $1 | 20 cents |
| | When fare is between $1 and $2 | 25 cents |
| | When fare is over $2 | 15% of fare |
| | In suburbs or country where many cabs have set fees or zone charges | No tip is necessary |
| | For extended set-fee trip | 15% to 20% of charge |

| WHO? | WHEN? | HOW MUCH? |
|---|---|---|
| **BEAUTY PARLORS** | | |
| Owner-operator | When he or she gives set | Generally no tip |
| | When he gives permanent, coloring, etc. | 10% of bill |
| Operator | When she does everything | 15% of bill |
| | When she shampoos only | 25 to 50 cents, depending on type of shop |
| Several operators | When one washes, one sets, one manicures, etc. | Divide 20% of bill in proportion to service given. |

# ENTERTAINING
## AND BEING
## ENTERTAINED

# 26 Party Preliminaries

Everyone, young people as well as adults, must do a certain amount of planning in order to give a successful party. Even if you decide at four o'clock to call some of the gang to come over and listen to records that evening, you have to make a few plans. You will, at the very least, have to:

Check with your parents to see if it will be all right.
Make sure that they will be at home to serve as chaperones.
Check the food and drink supply—and get whatever may be necessary.
Give some thought to your guest list. How many? Come alone or bring dates?

For this sort of really informal party, that's about it. Etiquette, and I, have very little to say because details take care of themselves. Everyone knows everyone else well, so it's not necessary to "get things moving," and all the hostess really need do is see that the Cokes and snacks don't run out, that no one person is left alone, and that the party doesn't get too noisy or too "cozy."

There are, of course, parties that need considerably more planning, and the material that follows will give you tips on how to go about it properly and efficiently.

## Invitations

Invitations to any but the most formal parties may be telephoned. A lot of people think this is the easiest way, but there are disadvantages. First, you rarely find everyone home when you first call, and that entails trying again and again. Second, the guests have no written reminder of the date, hour, etc., and people have been known to completely forget a telephoned invitation.

Written invitations should include:

Your name
The date and time
The place
The occasion, if it's a special one
The clothes to wear—whether it's casual or formal
The means of answering—you may put R.s.v.p. with a telephone number or address, or you may prefer to put "Regrets only" with your number.

The invitations may be written on your notepaper or informals, or calling cards if you have them.

Less formal, and I think more entertaining, are the colorful invitations available in all stationery stores. Pick one that is appropriate for the occasion, and fill in the pertinent information.

If you're clever and have the time, make your own illustrated invitations. The most original one I've seen lately was an invitation to a Christmas-tree-trimming party. The hostess had cut out little squares of paper of all colors and devised a collage of a tree. She made up a very witty poem that gave all the necessary information and included a request that each guest bring something foolish to add to the decorations.

If you are planning a formal party—dinner or dance—buy the engraved cards that follow the order of a formal engraved invitation, but which leave spaces for you to fill in names, dates, etc. Don't forget, when using this sort of card, to write the type of dress in the lower right corner. Written invitations should be sent at least ten days before the party.


## Your Guest List

How many? This really depends on two things—the size of your house or the place where the party will be held, and the amount you and your family can afford to spend. Consider both carefully: overcrowded rooms and lack of sitting space can ruin an otherwise good party, and if you exceed your budget your family won't be enthusiastic when you want to entertain again.

Date party or "singles"? If it is to be a "singles" party—boys and girls coming without dates—the hostess must plan on an even number, or, better still, an extra boy or two. She must also see that the guests mix, and that no one girl is left alone all the time. Since this can be very difficult if the party is large and includes people who do not know each other, most teen-agers prefer date parties. The invitations include a note "Bring a date," and they may be sent to boys only, or to both boys and girls. In the latter case, a girl is free to ask a boy to go with her. It must be clearly understood that this approval of a girl's asking a boy to be her date is limited to occasions when the invitation specifically requests it. It does *not* mean that manners and conduct have changed to the extent that girls should take over the boys' role on other occasions and become the inviters.

The guest receiving this kind of invitation should let the hostess know whom he or she is inviting, for it may be someone already invited, and that changes the hostess's estimate of the number she expects.

When a boy or girl is going steady, or has a previous date for the night of a "singles" party, it is not incorrect to call and ask if the date may be included. At the same time, if it makes too many people, or upsets the boy-girl ratio, the hostess has every right to refuse—politely and with an explanation, of course.

## Casual or Dress-Up?

Nine out of ten times you'll want your parties to be informal. It's a good idea to give *specific* instructions on the invitation—"jeans," "shirt and tie," "shorts or slacks," "skirts," mean much more than "informal" or "casual." Boys, especially, tend to be more relaxed in jeans and sweaters, but girls like them too. You can sit on the floor, play games, and dance more comfortably and modestly in slacks than in a short skirt.

However, when we asked teen-agers about clothes, seventy-five percent of you answered that you like to get dressed up every once in a while. So don't be afraid to plan a "jacket and tie" and "dress" party. Then dress up the party to suit the outfit—with fancier food, prettier decorations, and, perhaps, live music. The whole occasion takes on glamour that a "sloppier" party just doesn't have.

There are a few things that you should insist on, no matter *how* informal the party. Guests should arrive wearing shoes. They may kick them off later at *informal* parties, but at a formal dance girls should not be allowed on the floor without shoes. Say what you will, it lowers the whole tone of a formal party, and the tone is what makes such a party special. The same goes for jackets and ties: at a formal dance they must be kept on.

If an invitation says "black tie" or "formal," don't try to go unless that's what you're wearing. The hostess has set the tone of the party, so respect her wishes if you accept her invitation.

## What to Do?

There's no question about it, young people love to dance, so have some good records handy, and a cleared space. The most popular parties are those which combine the opportunity to dance with the opportunity to sit around and talk and eat. Boys, especially, like to take time out between dances to relax, but almost everyone enjoys a chance to sit down and talk about all sorts of things in a mixed group. It's a challenge to see if you can get a discussion started on some current school issue, or sports, or the moral questions that you ordinarily just talk about with your own sex.

Games are low on the list of popular party entertainment, but there are exceptions. Boys will almost always take to a pool or ping-pong table. In fact the former can be a hindrance—the girls may lose the boys for the entire evening. Ping-pong is safer, because boys and girls can play teams, or round robin.

A piano is a tremendous asset if one of the group can play, and I've never heard of a party that flopped when someone brought a guitar and started a song fest. A few physical games like "Twister" (a contortionist contest played by mixed teams, which is hilarious and strenuous) or carpet bowling are not to be scorned. If you can get one or two people to start a game, you'll find the whole group is soon ready to give it a try.

The old idea that it was necessary to have mixer games to get

things started has largely gone out of favor. Most of you, I'm sure, would prefer to sit in a corner and talk with one of your own friends rather than be forced into an artificial pairing-off. My recommendation, if things are slow and sticky, is to turn on the wildest record you have—at top volume—and I'll bet any amount it won't be three minutes before the party is swinging!

## Food and Drink

In thinking about food and drinks for your informal party, the only real problem is quantity. The worst calamity is to run short of drinks, so have on hand what you think you'll need, plus half again as much, and you'll be safe. After all, soft drinks keep indefinitely, and you and your family will use them up sooner or later. For an after-dinner party, count on your guests drinking two apiece, but also, I repeat, have extras in the refrigerator.

Speaking of the refrigerator, unless you have previously removed all the food that is not meant for your friends, make it clear that it is out of bounds. Many a father has gone down to the kitchen for a glass of milk, only to find the last drop gone. Put your party drinks in a tub of ice and place the tub in the room where the party is to be. Set up a table for snacks nearby. This will keep any but the most persistent prowlers out of the kitchen, and, if you suspect there are a few of them among your guests, hang an "out of bounds" sign on the refrigerator door.

Food for an after-dinner party is as simple as can be. Bowls of pretzels, popcorn, corn chips, and such are all that are necessary. Potato chips are good, but they do crumble badly and the bits that fall are greasy. If you're a good baker, homemade cake or cookies will make your refreshment table a special one. And if you and a couple of your friends want to cook up a batch of hot dogs or hamburgers around midnight, they're always a hit. Make the hamburger patties and butter the rolls ahead of time. If you're going to use frozen patties, be sure to remember to take them out of the freezer earlier. Your mother or father may be glad to help you with the late snack, and it's a good, unobtrusive way of letting your guests know there *are* adults around just in case the party starts to get a little out of hand. Other popular late-evening foods are pancakes (if you have a large enough griddle to be able to turn them out rapidly in quantity) or cheese fondue. The latter is delicious and unusual. Cover a card table with a plastic cloth (hot cheese drips) and melt the fondue, which can be bought canned or frozen, in a chafing or fondue dish. Before the guests arrive, cut a loaf of French bread into one-inch cubes, and keep them fresh by wrapping them in a damp cloth, foil, or plastic bag. When the time comes, serve the bread in a big basket beside the chafing dish. All you need to eat it with are forks, preferably the long fondue forks that are especially made for this dish. Everyone stands around and dips chunks of bread into the bubbling cheese. Serve plenty of paper napkins—though tasty and fun to eat, fondue is messy.

Pizzas are great late at night, too. If your town has a pizza parlor, ask your father or one of the boys to pick up freshly made ones at a specified hour. Don't forget to order them ahead of time. If you can't get fresh ones, some of the frozen pizzas are extremely good. Experiment with different brands beforehand and add touches of your own—sausage slices, olives, anchovies, or anything that appeals to you.

Your guests may well have had their fill of soft drinks by midnight, especially in cold weather, so with your late meal it's nice to serve pots of coffee or hot chocolate, and pitchers of milk.

# 27 Party Problems

## *Chaperones*

In looking over the answers to a questionnaire I sent out on the subject of chaperones, two very definite facts emerged, both of which bear out my firm conviction that teen-agers really want to do things the right way.

An overwhelming majority of you wrote that you think your parties *should* be chaperoned to some extent, and an equally large percentage told me that "most" parties in your area *are* chaperoned. You also gave me some very interesting and helpful information on the sort of chaperoning you think is necessary and desirable. From your ideas and my own knowledge of what is or isn't right, I think I can give you and your parents some answers to this question.

The ideal informal party chaperone is invisible most of the time but is *there*—awake and available if needed. Parents, of course, fill the role best, but any adult, or even a young married couple, will do. Chaperones should greet the guests when they arrive, thereby letting it be known they are on hand, and then they should go away to a bedroom, to a den—any place where they are out of sight. They should have a definite agreement with the host or hostess on what will and will not be allowed—for example, no lights out, no refrigerator raiding. Rather than having them wandering in and out to check on things, which puts an automatic damper on a party, the hostess should agree that she will immediately ask the chaperones for help if things get beyond her control.

Chaperones may put in an appearance to help serve refreshments —as I said in the last chapter, this is a good way of letting people know adults are around.

At large parties, such as dances, the chaperones—usually parents and their friends who have been enlisted to help, or committee members at subscription dances—should stay in evidence. They must, because big crowds require more attention, and the young hostesses are not able to keep an eye on everything themselves. The adults need not stay in the room with the dancers all the time, but they should be close by and should wander in and look around once in a while. The refreshment table is a handy and natural place for the adults to congregate and make themselves useful. At large dances, they may join the dancing occasionally; you all may even get a kick out of an exhibition of old-fashioned dancing, or watching Mom and Pop try out the new. At this sort of party, parents who are having a good time, and therefore not acting bored or disapproving, can add a great deal to the fun.

The fact that chaperones are on hand at an event does not imply that you are not to be trusted. They are there to help, not censure. No sensible young person wants a few unthinking guests to spoil a party, and you may at times need the authority of an adult to prevent this. The other reason for having chaperones is simply to protect your reputation and that of your friends. The adult world will assume, justly or not, that you're out for trouble if you refuse to put up with chaperoning. So why fight it? With an understanding between you and the chaperones, and some planning as to guests and activities, there is no reason for their presence to be more than a formality and a source of help in the unlikely event that it is needed.

## Crashers

There is a problem which, unhappily, is becoming more and more common—especially in the cities and suburbs. And there is no easy answer to it because the circumstances vary so much.

When your party is an "open house"—a really informal sort of come-on-over-tonight-and-bring-a-date type of party—the word may spread like wildfire. Rumor may turn it into "everyone's invited." At this sort of gathering, an uninvited guest really isn't a crasher, and the hostess is more or less obligated to let anyone in who is decently dressed and has an introduction through someone who was more specifically invited. *You should never let anyone into your home who is completely unknown to a single soul there.* If you don't want your party to turn into this sort of mob scene, you must issue more specific invitations, either by phone, in person, or in writing.

Assuming that invitations have been issued and you wish to, or must, restrict the number of guests, the problem becomes more difficult. Crashers are not likely to show up at small intimate parties. Chances are they won't hear of them; even if they do, they won't be interested. But let's say you're having an informal dance —maybe fifteen to twenty-five couples—and four nice-looking, well-dressed boys show up at the door. They tell you, "John Baxter [one of the invited guests present] is a friend of ours, and he said it would be all right if we came over." John Baxter actually was at fault; he had no business issuing an invitation in your name, and you have every right to tell them your party is big enough as it is and you just can't ask them in. If they get unpleasant about leaving, you can call your father, or whoever is chaperoning, to see that they leave. But do you really want to handle it that way? You certainly won't add to your list of friends, and there are few dances of any size that don't benefit from some extra males.

My opinion is that you would do well to invite John Baxter's friends in. *But* notice that I said "nice-looking, well-dressed" boys, who are vouched for *by someone at the party*. Suppose they were dirty, unshaven, dressed in jeans and sweat shirts, and gave no indication of knowing any of your guests—they had just "heard there was a party going on." *This* is the time to put your foot down. Send a friend to call your parents, if they're not nearby, because you'll probably need some adult authority around to get rid of this type of crasher. And stick to your guns even if some of your friends may vaguely know the boys, because they are the type who can wreck your party. They have no manners, no consideration, and no knowledge of how to act. If they start cutting in on your friends, hogging the food and drinks, and acting tough, real trouble can start between them and the invited boys.

In short, temper your dislike of the nerve and brashness of crashers with a little common sense. If they behave, and fit in with your friends, I would let them stay. Until, of course, the limit of guests you can accommodate has really been reached, or if you're serving a meal. In those cases you must be firm, but you can do it nicely. "We just can't squeeze another person in" or "I'm sorry but the steaks won't stretch for even one more." If you can succeed in getting them to leave without help, so much the better; if not, don't hesitate to call for an adult to assist.

In some areas, crashing has become such a problem that committees of subscription dances and parents of girls having debut or large formal parties hire a policeman or two to help control it. If this must be done, the policemen hired should be who are understanding and friendly with young people. They serve another useful purpose; at parties for older teen-agers where beer or liquor may legally be served, they can screen the boys as they leave to make sure that none of them has drunk too much to be able to drive safely. At a big party, they may also help with parking the cars. Often, just the presence of a man in uniform is enough to keep a party under control, and the crashers out of sight.

## The Question of Liquor

As long as there are teen-age parties, there will be boys who try to smuggle in liquor. In a recent survey we made, thirty-five percent of the boys and twenty-seven percent of the girls said that liquor was *sometimes* "sneaked in" and nineteen percent of the boys and sixteen percent of the girls claimed it was *often*. Very few said that it never happened.

This is wrong. In many of these cases it is not only wrong on moral and etiquette grounds—it is against the law.

You, as the hostess, have the responsibility for preventing it from happening at your party. It is usually a fairly easy thing to spot. At regular intervals, a group of boys will start edging out of a door, into the room where the men's coats are, or out to the kitchen. When they reappear, they're apt to be looking foolish, smug, or guilty. That is when you act. Without condemning the culprits—or apologizing—tell them that liquor is OUT. You have promised your parents that there will be no drinking, and the party will be cut short if there is. Ask them for your sake, and that of your other guests, to turn over the bottle or leave. If they don't hand it over at once, tell them you're going to get your father, and, if there's *still* a delay, do it. Your father can take the same tone and back you up. "Sorry, boys, but I made Betsy promise there would be no drinking if I let her have this party, so I'll have to ask you to let me keep the bottle until you leave, or else to go—with it —now." If the boys are of legal drinking age, the bottle should be returned at the end of the evening; if they are under age, your father should notify their parents, and turn the liquor over to them —not to the boys. As for serving liquor yourself, my advice to teen-agers when they ask me about it is—*don't do it*. If, despite the potential pitfalls and dangers, you do serve liquor, remember that not everyone likes or wants it, so always have plenty of soft drinks available.

## The Non-Mixers

At small come-on-over or date parties the problem of getting people to mix doesn't exist, but it certainly does when your group is big enough to include newcomers, or girls or boys who are not ordinarily members of your crowd.

There are some things a hostess can do to help this situation, whether the one on the sidelines is a stranger or just painfully shy. At a dance, have your date take time off from being your partner to ask a lonesome girl to dance, and then line up two or three other good friends to cut in on him. When you introduce your date to the girl—if she's a stranger to him—give her a lead to help her start a conversation: "John is the captain of the football team," or "Bill is just down from State U. for the weekend." This can be a great help to someone who is shy and at a loss to know where to begin.

Getting her started in this way is about all you can do; it's up to her to take it from there. If she's responsive, and at least a fair dancer, the boys you've sent to cut in may go back again, and her troubles will be over. The hostess must do her very best for her guest, but is not expected to continue nursing her all night. If she sees, later, that the girl is still left sitting alone, she can make one more try by asking her to join her own group for a snack or by introducing her to a boy who is also something of a stranger.

When a girl is really miserable at a dance, and all efforts to get her started have failed, she should call her parents, or a cab, and go home. Believe me, that is much less shattering or demeaning than being caught weeping in the ladies' room!

At just plain parties—some dancing, some chatting, some game playing—there are other things a hostess can do to help a sideliner. You can ask her to help you pass snacks or drinks; she'll *have* to circulate to do that. Draw her into the conversation if you can— "Ann had a funny experience the other day; tell them about it, Ann," or just ask her opinion on whatever you're talking about. If there is another stranger or shy person there—especially a boy— ask her to help *him* out. That's the greatest confidence builder in the world. When team games, such as round-robin ping-pong, are going on, be sure, even if you have to beg or bribe one of the captains, that she is chosen to play.

## Making Out

Unlike the problem of nonmixers, the problem of your party's becoming an excuse for making out is worse at date parties. Happily, this seems to be a problem only for the very young set. Just by getting older—and probably more serious—people increasingly prefer to make love in private.

But, if you think it may happen, there are three or four ways to avoid it, and the first is to choose your guests carefully. Don't invite *only* couples who are going steady. When you write out your list, mix it up. Inviting some heavy daters is fine, but also ask some people who you know are unattached; they will act as an automatic brake on the more ardent couples.

Keep *some* lights on. Turn them low for sitting around the fire or for dreamy dancing, but not all the way off. Your parents will object to total darkness, and it's perfectly legitimate to use them as an excuse—"Look, I've got to keep one or two lights on. Pop laid down the law—no lights, no party."

If the atmosphere seems dangerous, avoid too much mood music.

Keep plenty of refreshments flowing; you can always turn up the lights to pass a platter.

If you have a steady boy friend yourself, discuss things with him in advance. Tell him you don't want your party to turn into an "orgy," and you might need his help. For that night at least, he must put romance out of his mind and behave the way you want the other couples to act.

## Keeping the Curfew

When you issue your invitation, give an "until" time as well as an "at" time. Whether writing or telephoning, say "nine to twelve" or whatever the hours may be. That way, parents of nondrivers will show up to take them home, which will automatically start a breakup of the party.

Close up the food and drink supply a half hour or so before quitting time.

If it looks as though no one has any intention of leaving, enlist your best friends to help. "Mom and Dad are going to be furious if we don't break it up. Joe, would you mind starting the move?"

Failing all else, go and ask your parents to put in an appearance. This will do the job in a hurry!

# 28 Dinner Parties

## Formal Dinners

If you are giving a very formal dinner—before a debutante party or a prom, for instance—I'm sure your parents will provide help, most probably in the form of a catering service. In this event, you can leave everything except decorations, choosing the menu, and seating arrangements up to them. Fresh flowers are the loveliest of all table decorations. If you're not clever at arranging them, ask your mother or a talented friend to help you. The caterer will give you a choice of menus; choose one that has a wide appeal, *not* the most unusual or exotic. Finally, use place cards and seat your guests carefully; put congenial people together, and scatter strangers between those who know each other so that they will be included in general conversation.

## Do-It-Yourself Dinners

The dinner parties I want to discuss are those which you prepare yourself—from planning to cooking and serving. Of course you should go to your mother for advice—and help if she is willing to give it—but if you really do it yourself from soup to nuts, you'll get far more fun and satisfaction from it than if you're merely your mother's kitchen maid. Start out by making a list of all the equipment you'll need, the food you must buy, and any other reminders you may need, and keep the list in a handy spot where you can add to it or check items off as they are attended to.

The first time you give a dinner party, don't plan on more than three couples, including yourself and your date. If it's a success, try a larger party; but twelve people should be your maximum.

Do everything ahead of time that can possibly be done before the dinner, so that you can devote the evening to your guests and to having a good time yourself. It's awkward if you're in the kitchen, whipping cream or making gravy, as your friends are arriving. Casseroles and desserts can be made beforehand and frozen, salad greens can be washed, cut up, covered, and put in the refrigerator the night before. Then you need only put the casserole in the oven and add the dressing to the salad, which will take just a few seconds. Rolls or bread can be buttered and wrapped in foil and refrigerated a day ahead—all ready for last-minute heating. If you plan carefully, all you'll have to do on the day of the party (besides last-minute cooking chores), is to set your tables, arrange flowers or decorations, and see that the rooms you intend to use (including the bathroom) are immaculate.

## Menus

I am a great believer in two-course meals—entrée and dessert—when you're your own cook and maid. A casserole, no matter how complicated to prepare, requires no work once it is made, and is, therefore, an ideal main dish. If, however, you know that your friends don't consider it a real party unless they are served shrimp cocktail or vichyssoise first, have the shrimp or the soup on the table when the guests sit down.

I don't mean to imply that casseroles are the only meals you can have; there are roasts, fried chicken, delicious fish dishes, and so on. Just remember that roasts must be carved, gravies or sauces must be made at the last moment, and broiled fish or meat cannot be prepared in advance.

Consider eye appeal when you plan your meal. It's dull to serve breast of turkey with mashed potatoes and celery—they're all *white*. Don't serve creamed chicken, creamed potatoes, and puréed peas—they're all *runny*. The most successful meals combine a variety of colors and consistencies.

The following menus are chosen partly for their simplicity, but also because they are hearty, appetizing in appearance, and delicious. I'll be glad to provide the recipes if you'll write to me at the Emily Post Institute, 200 Park Avenue, New York, New York 10017.

*Chicken (or tuna fish), mushrooms, and noodle casserole*
*Croissants*
*Spinach salad (with bits of crisp bacon)*
*Apple pie and vanilla ice cream*

*Italian spaghetti and meat balls*
*Hard rolls*
*String beans with mushrooms (can be bought frozen)*
*Fruit compote and cookies*

*Lamb or beef stew (made with lamb, vegetables, and potatoes)*
*French bread*
*Lettuce and tomato salad*
*Ice cream and cake*

## The Dinner Table

Everybody has long since outgrown funny hats and snappers, so concentrate on making your table attractive without gewgaws. Just be sure that your décor fits the occasion and that all your accessories go well together.

If your dinner is a pre-dance party and the guests are coming in evening clothes, the table should be set formally. Use a white or lace tablecloth, rather than place mats, and the prettiest china and glass your mother will allow for the occasion. If it's a pre-debut dinner, the centerpiece should be white, or white and pink, but for other dinners your flowers may be of any color that goes well in the room.

For less formal occasions, the gayer the table, the better. For a dinner before or after a sports event—a school football or basketball game, for instance—choose tablecloths and napkins which tie in with your school colors. There's no reason not to use paper or plastic dishes and cups for informal parties. In fact, if you're going to rush off to a game after eating, what could be more practical than to throw these things out, leaving nothing but the silver to be washed later?

You can brighten your table by using checked tablecloths or mats for pizza parties or barbecues; gay flowered ones for dinners in spring and summer; orange, brown, and gold mats with a pumpkin or bowl of fruit instead of a flower centerpiece in the fall.

The china should be in keeping with the cloth you choose. If your cloth has a busy pattern, use solid-color plates, and vice versa. A lace cloth calls for delicate china; on a brown felt cloth, copper plates and mugs, or heavy beige or gold pottery look marvelous.

Don't be limited by the size of your dining-room table. If you want to have a party of twelve, and your table only seats eight, use three card tables, or put eight people at the main table and four at a card table nearby. Seat one of your good friends at each table other than your own, and ask her to act as hostess for that table. Your card tables need not be identical, but they should be similar enough to make a harmonious whole. An attractive effect can be attained by reversing colors at two tables—for example, yellow plates on an olive-green cloth at one, and the reverse at the other. To achieve harmony, put identical centerpieces and the same color candles—everyone loves to dine by candlelight—on both tables.

## Place Settings

All the silver that you need may be placed on the table, including the dessert spoons or forks. The order is simple. Forks go to the left of the plate, knives go to the right of the plate, with spoons to the right of the knives. Implements to be used first, except for knives, are placed furthest from the plate. The guests, if they are puzzled, simply start with the outside implement and work in. People from foreign countries put a dessert spoon *and* fork above each plate rather than beside it, and if you prefer to do that, it is not incorrect.

There is one exception to the rule of putting the fork on the left. The small shellfish fork is placed to the right of the spoons.

Spoons for coffee or tea are brought in on the saucers rather than being placed on the table.

Butter plates may be used at all but very formal dinners. The butter knife goes on the plate, pointing from lower right toward upper left with its blade toward the diner.

Large knives are put down so that the blade is facing the plate.

If plates or glasses are monogramed, be sure that the initials face the diner. Flowers or pictorial patterns on china should also be upright from the diner's point of view.

The napkin is folded as illustrated, and then placed in the center of the place setting. If a first course is already on the table when the guests arrive, the napkin is put on the left.

For the formal party, goblets are used for whatever beverage you serve. At less formal dinners, tumblers or highball glasses are fine.

Place cards go to the upper right or center of each place, or may sit on the folded napkin.

Salts and peppers should be placed so that they can be reached easily. Preferably there should be a set between every two places, but if you don't have enough to do that, put them at spots where the greatest number of people can reach them. If some of your guests smoke, don't forget the ash trays.

In front of the hostess's chair there should be heat-resistant mats for the serving dishes, and the utensils needed to serve the food.

To make serving simpler, salad on plates or in individual bowls may already be at the left of each place.

If there is to be a first course, that too is already on the table. Shrimp or fruit cocktail is usually served in a stemmed cup on a small plate. Soup may be served in small bowls or soup plates set on larger plates, or in two-handled cups on saucers.

## Seating Your Guests

You, as hostess, sit at the head of the table. If it's a square or a round table, choose for yourself the seat nearest the kitchen, and make that the head. The seat on your right goes to the male guest of honor. If you don't *have* a guest of honor, you must choose who sits there carefully. It may be your escort, but if it will help your seating arrangement, you can ask him to sit at another table or at the opposite end of your table to act as host. It may be the football hero at an after-game party, or it may just be someone you'd like to flatter a little by seating him next to you. In any case, the rest of your guests are seated whatever way you think they'll have the best time, alternating boys and girls. If you are six or twelve, a boy will be at the other end of the table; if you are four or eight, a girl will sit opposite you to maintain the boy-girl arrangement. If you don't use place cards, then you must tell the guests where to sit as they approach the table.

## Serving the Dinner

Just before you announce that dinner is ready—soon after everyone has arrived—you put the warmed plates and the dishes of food on the mats in front of your place.

You sit down at the same time as the guests, serve a plate, and pass it to your right, saying, "This is for Jack." Jack is seated at the opposite end of the table. You can, if you wish, serve each girl first, but it seems to go more smoothly if you work down the right side of the table, and then the left. As soon as three or four people are served, say, "Please start; don't let the food get cold."

Bread or rolls are on the table in a covered dish or basket, and the guests start to pass them around as soon as several people have their plates of food. The same is true of jellies or sauces.

When the hostess sees that two or three people are finished, she asks them if they would like second helpings.

It is a very good idea to have a hot plate or tray ready on a sideboard or nearby table so that you can place the platters and vegetable dishes on it when you have finished serving the first course. If you don't have a hot tray, you may take the serving dishes to the kitchen and put them in a warm oven.

When everyone is finished—not before—get up and remove the plates, two at a time. Don't stack dinner plates, but if there are butter dishes you may put one on each plate as you clear the places.

If there are only four or six people in all, tell the girls that you really don't need help. For more than six, let your best friend help you; and if you have three or four small tables, it's all right to ask one of the girls at each of them to clear that table. The same girls can help you serve dessert.

You may serve the dessert in exactly the same way as you did the main course, or you may put it on the plates in the kitchen and bring them in two at a time. If you are serving little cakes or cookies, they may be passed around the table by your guests after you give them their dessert plates.

When dinner is over, you must make the first move to leave the table. Push your chair back and start to get up; the others will follow suit.

## Semi-Buffet

Lots of people, myself included, prefer to serve dinner buffet style, if there are more than six or eight people. The dishes of food are put on a hot tray on a side table and the guests simply file by, serving themselves. Then they take their plates of food to places set at the dining-room table or several small tables. From there on it's a regular sit-down dinner. Dessert is generally served already placed on the plates, or at each table—not buffet style.

## Buffet Dinners

At a full buffet dinner you can entertain as many people as your equipment and house can accommodate. Guests serve themselves to all parts of the meal, and sit any place they wish—including on the floor or the stairs.

### THE BUFFET TABLE

If your party is large, use your dining-room table and put it in the center of the room so that two lines of guests may serve themselves at once. If you do not have a dining room, arrange two card tables or a big kitchen table, covered with tablecloths, at the end of the living room. Stacks of plates and silver are divided into two parts and placed at either end. Study the diagram below for an ideal buffet setup.

For a smaller party, the table may be placed against a wall, so that the guests will pass by in one direction. Remember to arrange plates and silver at the end of the table nearest the entrance, or the spot the guests approach first.

Beverages and glasses or cups, because of the space problem, should be on a separate table in the same room.

The table may be as formal or informal as the occasion demands. Just as at a sit-down dinner, damask and crystal are appropriate for a debut dinner, pottery and pewter are fine for an informal occasion. What really makes your table attractive is your skill in combining colors and materials.

## THE BUFFET MENU

Hot dishes should be served in chafing dishes, and cold dishes should be sliced or carved into serving portions ahead of time. An ideal buffet offers some of each. The menus suggested below are not difficult and they offer variety and choice of popular foods.

*Platter of cold sliced meats*
*(ham, turkey, roast beef, cold cuts)*
*Scalloped potatoes*
*Vegetable salad*
*Rolls*
*Ice cream bricks and cookies*

*Beef Stroganoff*
*Noodles*
*Green salad*
*French bread*
*Fresh fruit, cheese and crackers*

*Shrimp casserole*
*Rice*
*Green peas*
*Croissants*
*Chocolate mousse*

Dishes of condiments, nuts, and jellies may be placed on the buffet table, too.

# 29 Debuts

The original idea of a debut, or coming-out party, was to announce to the world that one's daughter was of marriageable age and ready to be introduced to eligible men. Until the day she "came out," a belle of long ago was chaperoned within an inch of her life and barely had the opportunity to speak to, much less be alone with, members of the opposite sex.

Nowadays your coming-out season is really just an excuse to be invited to loads of parties and possibly to have one of your own. But it still does serve the purpose of allowing a girl to widen her circle of friends and get to know many boys she might otherwise never meet.

## Group Debuts

Far more common than a private debut is the less-expensive and simpler process of coming out as a member of a group. These parties may be called assemblies, cotillions, or balls, and they are run by committees who decide which girls will be invited to come out under their auspices. The ball may be a charity benefit, or the fees charged each girl may simply be used to keep the affair self-sustaining.

A debutante's parents or grandparents may wish to give a private party in addition to the group debut, and this often takes the form of a dinner given before the ball. It may be completely separate, however—a tea, a tea dance, or another ball.

At group debuts, the receiving line, which the parents and guests must go through, is made up of members of the committee. The girls do not form a receiving line if it is a large group; instead, they are presented *to* the committee and to their mothers by their fathers. At many parties the fathers and daughters rehearse quite intricate figures which they perform as part of this ceremony.

Each debutante asks two or more boys to be her escorts, often choosing a brother or cousin for one, if they are friends. She must show no favoritism, and must give equal time to each all evening. When one is a relative, he may tactfully bow out and leave the other as her date for parties afterward, or when it is time to see her home. The other guests are invited in various ways: at some parties each family is given a limited number of invitations to issue themselves; at others the postdebutantes from the previous year are invited, and allowed one or two escorts each. Some committees invite additional boys and girls themselves; others do not.

Debutantes almost invariably wear white, and the committee may dictate certain regulations—for example, short or long dresses (according to the current style), no tight skirts, no strapless dresses, etc. The girls wear long white gloves, and carry identical bouquets. The escorts and the debutantes' fathers usually wear white tie and tails. Other male guests wear tuxedos.

All the details—photographers, refreshments, flowers, etc.—are handled by the committee that runs the ball, and all the girl and her parents need do is adhere to the rules and pay the fee.

## Private Debuts

Your town may not have any of these group debuts, or your parents may prefer to give you a coming-out party of your own. Unless you have a very large home, it is usually held at a club or hotel, and this relieves your parents of the details of food, service, and so on. However, you and they will have to plan the decorations and the menu, and hire the photographer, the orchestra, and any additional entertainment.

You, your mother, and possibly your grandmother form the receiving line. Your father stays near the line greeting people separately, introducing them, and acting as a host. Generally the receiving line stands against a background of greens and flowers, many of them sent by the guests. Your escort should stay nearby much of the time to run errands or bring you refreshments.

When it is time to break up the line—after most of the guests

have arrived and already started to dance—the debutante has her first dance, with her father, and the others clear the floor to watch and applaud. One of her escorts cuts in, Father begins to dance with Mother, and then the guests join in.

Since the dates for coming-out parties are limited to vacation periods when most young people are home, two or even more girls may choose the same date for their debuts. If the guest lists overlap badly, the girls may wish to combine their parties. A very satisfactory solution is for one to give a dinner dance at seven-thirty or eight, and the other a ball starting at ten or eleven.

At the later party, a supper is always served between twelve-thirty and one o'clock. A chef may be grilling hamburgers, a cook may be turning over pancakes and frying sausages, or there may be chafing dishes of creamed chicken or scrambled eggs. If you wish, it can be a much simpler meal of sandwiches or sliced hams and turkeys. Whatever the food, coffee is usually served.

Family friends often send gifts, and many people send flowers. The deb's escorts are expected to send corsages, her father usually does, and she may receive many more. She should wear those given her by her escorts—if possible. One way to avoid hurt feelings is to pin all your corsages to a wide white satin or velvet ribbon and tie this around your wrist. It cannot be worn while you're dancing, of course, but it looks beautiful in photographs and while you are standing in the receiving line. Otherwise, extra corsages should be displayed with the other flowers behind the line.

On this occasion above all others—when a girl is supposed to show the world that she has become an adult—it is important that she write thank-you letters immediately to each and every person who has sent a gift or flowers.

# 30 House Parties

## *Invitations*

A hostess may invite house-party guests by phone, note, or word-of-mouth, but she should be sure to include the following information:

> The date and time of day she would like her guests to arrive.
> The same facts for when she expects them to leave.
> Information on how to get there—train or plane schedules; directions for driving.
> Her address and phone number.
> Some indication of the activities planned, and suggestions about any special clothing needs.

The only requirement for a guest is that the reply be made promptly, and in writing if the invitation was written. Either with the acceptance, or as soon as definite plans are made, the hostess should be notified at what time, and by what means, one intends to arrive.

When a boy wants a girl to visit him, even for one night, his mother should write her a note. If this formality has been overlooked, Janie's mother naturally wonders whether to let her go. In that case, Janie may perfectly well ask the young man to remind his mother that a confirmation is in order. Should this all happen at the last minute, with panic setting in on all sides, his mother may call Janie's mother on the phone and put things right.

## *Dos and Don'ts for the Hostess*

(I would include "host," but if a boy gives a house party in his family's home, his mother usually takes care of the details of making guests comfortable. But he should, of course, take the same pains as a hostess would to plan activities and see that his guests have a good time.)

An ideal hostess:

1. Sees that the rooms allotted to her guests, have:

   Beds made up with fresh sheets, and, in winter, plenty of covers.
   A luggage rack or a table or stool to serve as one.
   Empty hangers in the closet.
   At least one empty bureau drawer for each guest.
   Water glass in the bathroom.
   Clean towels and washcloths—preferably in colors different from the
      family's and from each other's.
   Facial tissues.
   Nice but not essential—a radio, a clock, something to read (maga-
      zines or short stories), safety pins, reading light by bed.

2. Has plenty of soft drinks and snacks readily available so the guests can help themselves.
3. Explains household routines that the guests should know about —especially breakfast. If there is no maid and meal hours are flexible, let people sleep late unless, of course, a special activity is planned. Have a pitcher of juice and a pot of coffee ready in the kitchen, and leave out in plain sight the ingredients and utensils for a more substantial breakfast. The hostess may even leave a note: "Get yourself something to eat and come on down to the beach—Jane and I are sunbathing!"
4. Makes reservations ahead of time for:

   Theater seats
   Tennis courts
   Dinner in a restaurant
   Club dances
   Any special activity or entertainment that requires tickets

5. Introduces her guests whenever they meet her friends from that area.
6. Keeps any annoyances hidden from guests. Whether the dish-washer breaks down, or one of the boys breaks her record player,

a good hostess keeps a smile on her face until the last guest has left.

7. Plans some specific activities, but leaves some free time. Guests enjoy relaxing.

## Dos and Don'ts for Guests

I suppose the best way to judge your popularity as a guest is whether you're asked back again. You, or your mother, must have said, on occasion, "I'll never have *him* in the house again!" Or, in a happier vein, "That Bill is wonderful—he can come *any* time!" If you can honestly say you follow the guidelines listed below, you'll be pretty sure to fall into the latter category.

The ideal guest:

1. Goes home when she planned, even if urged to stay.
2. Conforms to the household's habits. If your hostess says breakfast will be at nine in the dinette, *don't* say, "Can't I skip breakfast and sleep instead?"
3. Plans her packing *carefully* so that she doesn't have to borrow continually from the hostess and other guests. Sports equipment, cosmetics, things like nail files and safety pins, extra stockings in case of a run, gloves are often-forgotten items.
4. Keeps her room neat. Makes the bed as soon as she gets up unless specifically told that a maid will do it. Keeps the bathroom sink clean.
5. Does not ask friends she meets or new acquaintances to her hostess's house, *nor* does she accept invitations for herself or the whole group without consulting the hostess.
6. Offers to help *immediately and cheerfully* with any household chores—tidying, preparing meals, or washing up after them.
7. Joins into any activity with enthusiasm.
8. Does not raid the refrigerator without permission.
9. Doesn't use the telephone without asking first, and never makes a long-distance or charge call without getting the cost from the operator and giving the money to her hostess's mother immediately.
10. Is careful to take home everything she brought so that her

hostess doesn't have to be bothered with returning various items.

11. When leaving, strips the bed and puts the bedspread back on; leaves the room as neat as she found it.

12. Tips the maid if there is one. Anyone who has done any cooking for you, or cleaned your room, thereby having extra work to do, should receive $2 after a weekend visit. Give it to her personally, with a friendly remark: "Thanks a lot, Eve. Your meals were great."

13. Thanks the hostess and her parents when she leaves, and *also* writes a thank-you note to the parents within three days. (See chapter on "Letters That Must be Written" for samples.)

14. Takes a house present to her hostess's mother. A new novel, a record if the family enjoys music and has a record player, a kitchen gadget for a gourmet cook, or a plant which may be put in the garden after it blooms is always appreciated. Although candy is popular if there are younger brothers and sisters, so many women are weight-watchers now that I don't think it's the best choice of a gift. You do not need to take a gift to your own friend, nor, if she's a very close friend, do you need to write her a special thank-you note.

To sum up, the popular guest—the one who *will* be asked back time and again—has four qualities: adaptability, consideration, enthusiasm, and appreciation.

# 31 Special Parties

Some people are natural party givers; others are not. But, if you accept invitations from your friends regularly, it's only fair to return the compliment—and it *is* a compliment—occasionally.

Your own inclination, your family situation, or perhaps the facilities of your home may make it difficult for you to be a spur-of-the-moment hostess. In that case, you probably don't entertain often, so make the occasions when you do a little extra special. I won't go into detailed descriptions of various types of parties, but will give you a few hints or suggestions about some that are easy to plan—and fun too.

## Costume Parties

Have a theme. It may be a party to celebrate a holiday or it may be something as simple as "Come as you were when you received the invitation."

Most males feel silly "dressing up," so choose a theme which lends itself—at least for them—to simple additions or alterations to normal clothing.

Offer prizes—one for boys, one for girls, and one for best couple or group. People *will* try harder if you make it worthwhile.

## TV Parties

Get together to watch a football bowl game, a World Series game, or the Kentucky Derby.

Offer a prize for the best guess on the final score, order of finish, or whatever fits.

Serve cold chicken-in-a-basket with potato chips on gaily colored cardboard trays, which are available at stationery and party-supply stores. Prepare the trays ahead of time and pass them around yourself, or with your best friend's help, so your guests won't have to leave the game.

## Outdoor Barbecues

Get an agile boy to put floodlights high up in several trees surrounding the patio or barbecue area. A romantic effect can be achieved by pointing them upward into the branches, rather than shining them down into people's eyes. If there are steps around, stick "mushroom" lights or flares beside them to prevent accidents.

Beg, borrow, or buy a really *big* garbage pail for used paper plates, cups, etc. It will save you a lot of work the next day.

Most important—have an alternate place for the party ready in case of bad weather.

## Birthday Parties

Help guests by suggesting silly gifts only—with say, a fifty-cent limit —or by asking for a fifty-cent contribution to a gift you know the guest of honor really wants. The hostess makes the purchase, and she gets all the guests to sign the gift card.

Do have an old-fashioned birthday cake! Most people are secretly disappointed when this formality is overlooked.

## Progressive Parties

These parties provide a good way for several girls to share expenses and responsibilities.

A three-course dinner is best, because *too* much moving from house to house gets boring. Tomato juice with hors-d'oeuvre, or fruit cocktail, or shimp is served at the first house. The second hostess provides the main course, and the third serves the dessert. The last house should be the one most suitable for dancing, or for whatever you want to do the rest of the evening. If you want a fourth member in the hostess group, the party can move on once more, and this girl provides the after-dinner drinks and snacks. Otherwise, these too are served by the one who does the dessert. All of the party costs are added up and divided evenly.

## Card Parties

Poker or Twenty-one can be loads of fun—even with no real gambling involved. Use fake paper money or regular chips and pay off the winner with a prize.

If any in your group are learning to play bridge, try a bridge party. If your mother plays, ask her to help out, and offer a small prize to the winners at each table.

Set a time limit for all card parties. They are hard to break up, but you can enforce the cut-off by starting to serve food a few minutes before "closing time."

## After-Skiing, After Skating

The main ingredients for these get-togethers are a roaring fire and hot food and drink.

As a change from coffee and chocolate, try a big tureen of steaming soup. Or serve meat fondue. Set up a table near the fire with the following things:

A fondue pot or chafing dish in the center, filled with hot cooking oil.
A big tray of chunks of beef, pieces of chicken liver, and sausage.
A tray of sauces—mustard, Russian dressing, ketchup, sweet and sour sauce.
A bowl of potato chips or sticks.
Fondue forks, napkins, and paper plates.

This is a do-it-yourself meal. Everyone gathers around, spears a chunk of meat, and cooks it to his liking in the oil—a matter of thirty seconds or so. The plates provide a place for the meat to cool for a minute before being eaten. Guests may either dip the meat into the bowls of sauce, or put a little of each sauce onto their plates.

Have boxes of marshmallows ready for toasting in the fireplace. They make a fine dessert, and long kebab skewers are handy for spearing them.

## Beach Parties

Beach parties are the best fun of all in the summer. Most of them are Dutch treat—a group simply decides it's a good night for a beach party, and anyone who hears about it goes. They're usually more successful, however, if two or three girls and boys take charge —to organize wood-gathering details, to see that there is charcoal for cooking, to get the permission of the town authorities to build a fire, etc.

There's no reason not to host a beach party yourself, meaning you provide the food and drink as well as assuming the chores mentioned above. Here are some suggestions that will help your picnic run smoothly.

Check out your picnic spot early in the day, and do whatever policing is necessary.

Choose a spot that affords privacy, but which is not so far from civilization that you can't go or send a friend for anything essential that may have been forgotten.

Get a couple of friends (preferably male) to help you collect the wood for the bonfire.

Offer something different from the usual hamburgers or hot dogs. Shish kebabs (chunks of lamb or beef on skewers with a variety of vegetables between) prepared in advance grill beautifully over coals. So do lamb chops, baked potatoes or corn wrapped in foil, and cut-up chicken parts.

Stick to "finger foods." All of the above can be eaten without benefit of knife and fork, as can any type of sandwich, of course.

If you prefer hamburgers, butter the rolls and make the patties at home. It's much more convenient at the kitchen table, and there's no danger of losing anything in the sand.

Burn up burnable trash, but *don't* throw bottles, cans, or foil into the fire. Take an extra paper bag or two to carry them home or to the nearest garbage can.

When you're ready to leave, douse your fire with water, or, if it is not near anything flammable, let it burn out. Don't bury it; too many people have been severely burned by stepping on the red-hot sand covering the coals.

\*        \*        \*

Very possibly you think there are too many dos and don'ts in this book, and you may ask yourself, "Why should I conform to these rules?" We all know that the world facing us is changing enormously and rapidly. There is a tendency, and not only in your generation, to feel that today's ideas, standards, and morals are outdated and unacceptable. I am not going to enter this debate, but I would like to discuss a very real problem that it raises. Any standard you reject must be replaced with another of your own choosing. It's important to remember that the specific rules, the actual dos and don'ts, are important, but they are not as important as the thinking process behind them.

Consideration—the basis of etiquette—insight and understanding, self-control and discipline, loyalty, and finally a sense of justice are the timeless qualities that make life rewarding and pleasant.

There is not a single "rule" or even suggestion given in this book that is not related to one of these characteristics. Learning to live by these guidelines is in itself a form of self-discipline, and it provides the self-assurance essential to happiness and success. You will have to create your own interpretations as you grow older and as society changes. But if the basic standards of etiquette—today's etiquette—have become a part of you, you will be better prepared for the future. If you have accepted and learned from the discipline that a knowledge of correct behavior imposes, you will be able to take your part, with confidence, in whatever type of society emerges in the coming years.

# Index